Golf

second edition

GOLF
building a solid game

Gary Wiren

PGA Master Professional

Prentice Hall, Englewood Cliffs, New Jersey 07632

Library of Congress Cataloging-in-Publication Data

Wiren, Gary.
   Golf : building a solid game / Gary Wiren. — 2nd ed.
     p. cm.
   Includes bibliographical references (p.) and index.
   ISBN 0-13-359100-X
   1. Golf.   I. Title
GV965.W72 1992
796.352 '3—dc20
                                90-26987
                                    CIP

Acquisitions Editor: *Ted Bolen*
Editorial/production supervision
  and interior design: *Mark Tobey*
Cover design: *Patricia Kelly*
Prepress buyer: *Herb Klein*
Manufacturing buyer: *Patrice Fraccio*

© 1992, 1987 by Prentice-Hall, Inc.
A Simon & Schuster Company
Englewood Cliffs, New Jersey 07632

Printed in the United States of America
10 9 8 7 6 5 4 3 2 1

ISBN   0-13-359100-X

Prentice-Hall International (UK) Limited, *London*
Prentice-Hall of Australia Pty. Limited, *Sydney*
Prentice-Hall Canada Inc., *Toronto*
Prentice-Hall Hispanoamericana, S.A., *Mexico*
Prentice-Hall of India Private Limited, *New Delhi*
Prentice-Hall of Japan, Inc., *Tokyo*
Simon & Schuster Asia Pte. Ltd., *Singapore*
Editora Prentice-Hall do Brasil, Ltda., *Rio de Janeiro*

To Ione, the rosy-cheeked girl in the "Old G."
Still rosy-cheeked thirty years later.

CONTENTS

7

THE SHORT GAME
where score can be influenced most quickly   72

8

RULES AND ETIQUETTE
golf's laws and manners   84

9

GETTING OUT TO PLAY
testing what you have learned   98

10

PRACTICE
the way to success   107

PREFACE

"Why do you want to learn the game of golf?" I've asked hundreds of beginners this question, and I've received such answers as: "Our company has an annual tournament and almost everyone else plays;" "I've watched it on T.V. and it looked interesting;" "My husband is a golf nut and I'm tired of staying home;" or simply, "It looks like fun." All these answers share one thing in common: Each person is looking for satisfaction and enjoyment. The first part of this book is addressed primarily to the elementary golfer. It assumes that the reader has little or no golf experience, so novices: Feel comfortable. The text's fresh treatment of golf's fundamentals, however, will provide a valuable review for the more experienced player. In addition, the second portion of the book will take the reader well beyond the novice stage. In other words, this book will appeal to all levels of golfers.

If you are not a golfer at present but intend to become one, you will join millions of other sportsmen and women throughout the world who have found this game a fascinating and enjoyable outdoor activity. The information contained in this book will help you make all your experiences in golf more pleasant and rewarding.

Gary Wiren

Golf

1

GOLF

what to expect

Before you invest both time and effort in learning the game of golf, this chapter will tell you:
1. What the game of golf expects of you.
2. What you may reasonably expect to receive in return.

Golf is a game that is meant to be enjoyed; it can be a vivid test of emotion and skill. This is the first principle that the new golfer should understand. But never let the test become so serious that you lose sight of the fact that enjoyment should be your number one goal.

If you aren't sure what to expect from golf or know whether you'll like it, just ask yourself the following questions. Do I have an active imagination? Do I have a desire to meet new people? Do I like to be outdoors in beautiful surroundings? (Figure 1–1) Do I relish a challenge? If you can answer "yes," then congratulations on your choice of activities—golf will serve you well. This chapter will discuss some of the personal requirements that you will need to participate in golf successfully. It will also list some of the game's rewards and limitations. In order to judge the value of golf as an activity for you, you should begin to formulate some questions about the game's positive and negative features.

PERSONAL NEEDS

A question certainly worth asking is, What personal qualities do I need to play golf? Assuming that you want to know those attributes possessed by the more than twenty-five million golfers in this country, here are the basic personal requirements.

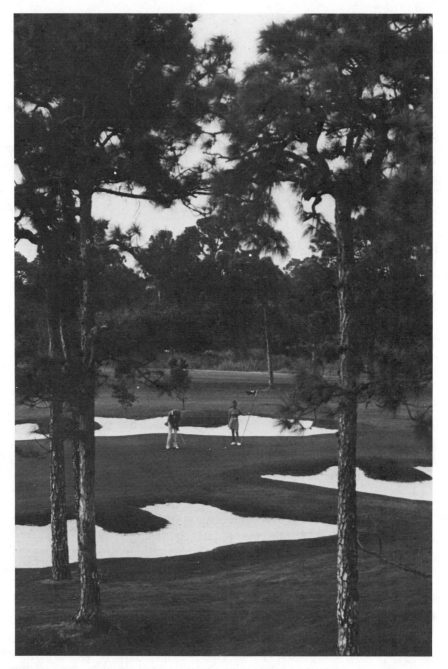

Figure 1–1
The beauty of golf's surroundings helps make it a relaxing out-of-doors sport
experience.

Motor Skills

Previous success in other sports could make the game easier to learn yet it does not necessarily ensure success in golf. You needn't be a great athlete to enjoy the game. The "natural athletes" are sometimes discouraged because they are unable to master the game in a few sessions. On the other hand, the less physically adept persons who have to work hard for their results often accept temporary failure as a natural step in learning. With continued practice their results are often better than those of their more talented counterparts. Naturally, the more physically talented and better coordinated you are, the greater initial potential you possess. But our finest golf champions acknowledge that desire and work are still two of the greatest attributes which lead to success in the game.

Physiological

Golf is not designed to severely tax the human physiological makeup. People of all sizes and degrees of physiological composition have found satisfaction and success in the game. Most people require no special conditioning or training to play. This is not to say that good physical conditioning may not aid your performance—it certainly can—but to simply participate, that is, to walk nine or eighteen holes and hit your shots, does not usually require special physical conditioning. Some people might find it difficult to complete an eighteen-hole round of golf because they lack the stamina; but for most participants, the walk and mild exercise can prove to be more invigorating than taxing. If you possess greater than average strength and size, and at least normal flexibility, you may have an advantage over other golfers at your level. But golf lessens some of the physical differences in individuals by requiring not only strength for achieving good distance, but also a sense of "touch" for accuracy and adeptness in shorter strokes around the greens. In short, the physical requirements needed for participation in golf are few, and certainly not overwhelming.

Psychological

The psychological qualities most necessary for enjoyable and successful participation in golf are *patience, concentration,* and a *sensible approach* to failure and success. You need patience to put in the necessary hours of practice even when you see little improvement. Concentration on the task at hand—swinging the club—is an obvious essential. A strong belief in your abilities is also necessary for producing your best performance. Above all, you must have the right attitude toward early failures, otherwise frustration will completely spoil the enjoyment of the experience as well as interfere with the learning process. Golf can be a source of relief from tension and stress, but it can also be a severe test of one's emotional control. Two emotions commonly displayed in the game are *fear* and *anger*. Your ability to cope with these two emotions will certainly affect your success and personal pleasure in golf.

The nervousness you may feel as you tee your first ball and prepare to swing in the presence of others is caused by a fear of not performing well—an emotion experienced by even the finest and seemingly most composed players. It's only natural to feel a little nervous when about to perform, but this can have devastating effects if a player allows the importance of the act to get out of perspective. Fear causes tension, and tension can prevent a good swing. If you experience this apprehension in your early games, it is usually temporary and will diminish when you begin to develop more confidence in your swing and ability. Tension will be further reduced when you fully understand that you are there on the course for enjoyment. You must, therefore, also put your results in the proper perspective.

Expressing anger while playing is self-defeating. Golfers who can't control their anger leave the course with more tension than they had when they came. If you play so badly that you get angry enough to vow to do some practicing, then anger can be useful—it is then "channeled correctly." But if your anger over a misplayed shot eliminates all pleasure in the game, you defeat the initial purpose of being on the course—to have fun, to *play*. Thus, the "play-for-fun" golfer should possess enough self-discipline to control the tension that could result from fear or anger lest it spoil her or his recreation. If you have developed the ability to approach frustrating circumstances philosophically, then you will have overcome one of the tougher psychological challenges of golf.

GOLF'S REWARDS

Social Opportunities

Golf has a built-in socializing system. Besides the sponsored golf activities that allow people to mix in any well-run golf club program, there is the universal tradition of pairing players who come to the course alone looking for a game. One man who has played at a local public links for thirteen years has never come to the course with a partner, yet has always managed to find a game and has made hundreds of acquaintances through his golfing activity. Recently I was paired in Canada with a visiting Houstonian, a man who has played golf in seventy-five countries, in every state capital of the United States, and in every British Commonwealth country that has a course with the title "Royal" attached to its name. He travels almost exclusively alone but always manages to find a game—and with it a wealth of acquaintances. You may not be quite this adventuresome, but you can find many new friends through golf if you desire. Friendships made through golf can turn out to be some of the closest in your life.

Physical and Mental Conditioner

The contribution golf can make to your physical fitness depends upon such factors as whether you ride or walk around the course, the speed at which you walk if you do, and whether you carry your own clubs. Basically, an eighteen-hole round of golf on foot is equivalent to a four and one-half- or five-mile walk with intermittent stops. It is a moderate form of exercise, having aerobic value that can leave you feeling exhilarated from being outdoors.

An equally important contribution toward health and well-being is the game's potential for relieving psychological tension. Physicians have been known to recommend the game as a prescription for irritability and chronic fatigue caused by tension. Whether or not golf relieves tension is strictly dependent upon one's personality and attitude toward the game. For people who have the wrong perspective on why they are there, a round of golf actually can increase tension. In most cases, however, it is a valuable aid to relaxation, eagerly anticipated and enjoyed by millions.

Lifetime of Activity for All Ages

You can look forward to playing golf throughout your lifetime. John D. Rockefeller played regularly even after his ninetieth birthday, while an equally famous person, Arnold Palmer, began playing at the age of five. This wonderful age span makes the game an excellent family activity. One family in the United States has an annual golf outing and putting championship at which a trophy is awarded. The participants bridge four generations. A surprise winner in one putting contest was an eighty-four-year-old grandmother—now that's a family sport! It's no wonder that golf has been called "the game of a lifetime."

Probably the greatest tribute to golf and the best explanation of what you can expect from this game was fashioned by D. R. Forgan:

A Tribute to Golf
It is a science, the study of a lifetime, in which you may exhaust yourself but never your subject.
It is a test of temper, a trial of honour, a revealer of character.
It affords a chance to play the man and act the gentleman.
It means going into God's out-of-doors, getting close to nature, fresh air exercise, a sweeping away of the mental cobwebs, genuine recreation of the tired tissues.
It is a cure for care—an antidote to worry.
It includes companionship with friends, social intercourse, opportunity for courtesy, kindliness, and generosity to an opponent.
It promotes not only physical health but moral force. (Forgan, 1935, Frontispiece)

IS GOLF THE RIGHT ANSWER?

Although golf has helped to fill the need for exercise and fun for millions of people in the world, it isn't the answer for everyone. Some have tried the game and quit; others have felt that golf wasn't what they wanted. Why?

Golfing takes time—more time than many people have. Whereas you would consider two hours spent playing tennis, badminton, or handball to be a good overall workout, it takes the average American about twice that time to complete a round of golf—and even longer in some metropolitan areas where the demand for golf facilities is great. In such cases it is not uncommon for a weekend golf outing (including the time it takes for getting to the course, waiting to get on the course, and playing) to stretch into an eight-hour ordeal. In Japan it could be sixteen hours!

Humankind is finding an ever-increasing amount of leisure time available in this day and age, but for some there's not yet enough time for golf. If time is a problem, consider that there are millions of nine-hole rounds of golf played in this country annually. A two-hour nine-hole round is just right for many; plus, under good conditions you can still find places where the three- to three and one-half-hour eighteen-hole round is played.

In addition to this, golf costs money. When compared to skiing, boating, hunting, and other activities, it can be relatively inexpensive; but for many budgets golf is simply out of reach. Greens fees, balls, and other minor accessories are ongoing expenses after the initial price of clubs, bag, and shoes has been met. If a person needs to make a choice which depends heavily on economy, he or she probably should be aware of some cost-saving ideas such as buying used rather than new equipment (both clubs and balls) and frequenting municipal courses where greens fees are modest.

Also, although golf can be a great test of skill, it is not essentially a serious test of one's physiological condition. A weekly game of eighteen

Figure 1–2
Golf cars are a big source of revenue but spoil one of the best reasons for playing—the walk.

holes for instance, is not enough exercise for a healthy person under retirement age. As a moderate form of activity, however, it is of worth to the otherwise sedentary individual. But regular use of a golf car, can destroy the exercise needed to maintain a state of physical well-being. (Figure 1-2) If you play three to five times a week, hit practice balls, and walk during your rounds, that's a different story.

It is only fair that you realize from the beginning that golf, although a great game for many, can have some shortcomings and limitations. Try to steer clear of them. Hopefully you will find the game's liabilities not serious enough to prevent you from discovering its many assets.

AFTER READING THIS CHAPTER YOU SHOULD KNOW THAT:

The physical requirements needed to play the game of golf should not deter the "play-for-fun" participant.

Golf affords a psychological challenge that can test and/or help one learn to control one's emotions.

Golf is a social, recreational activity that can provide needed relaxation for people of all ages.

When compared to other individualized sports, golf can be classified as moderately expensive and above average in the expenditure of leisure time.

Millions of golfers continue to find great enjoyment through their participation.

2

GOLF, THE GAME_____

then and now

In this chapter you will be introduced to:
1. *Golf's origin, development in the United States, and effect on our culture.*
2. *The right attitude with which to face the game's challenges.*
3. *Basic features of the course, scorecard, and club design.*

Golf has been called the Royal and Ancient Game. Deservedly so, for it can be traced to the fifteenth century when it was played by kings, queens, and noblemen. Records also indicate that university students at St. Andrews in Fife, Scotland, played golf as early as 1415. Games similar to golf, however, were played even earlier than the fifteenth century in Asia, South America and Holland. A ball-and-stick game somewhat similar to golf, called *paganica*, was played at the time of the Roman Empire. But golf as we know it was popularized, if not invented, by the Scots.

EARLY GOLF IN THE UNITED STATES

Although records indicate that golfers' meetings were held in the United States as early as the 1600s and that golf was played in several regions early on, the first officially established golf course in this country still in existence is in the town of Yonkers, New York. Built in the year 1888 and appropriately named the "St. Andrews Club," it was a crude three-hole, later six-hole, and finally eighteen-hole layout which bore a striking resemblance to a cow pasture—which is exactly what it was. By 1900, twelve short years later, there were 1,000 courses in the United States, and five U.S. Opens, five U.S. Amateurs for both men and women, and three intercollegiate championships had been held. Every state in the Union had a golf course; the game was definitely on its way.

Although facilities were being built at a startling rate, golf was still considered to be a "rich man's sport." The finest players of the early 1900s were well-to-do people who had ample leisure time to practice and play. The average American considered golf to be a foreign game played by millionaires, and to a certain extent this was true. But in 1913, at the Country Club of Brookline, Massachusetts, an unheralded twenty-year-old local caddie named Francis Ouimet defeated the best players America had to offer, including the greatest golfers of the British Isles, Harry Vardon and Ted Ray. Ouimet thus became the first player born in this country to win the U.S. Open. With a new homebred champion, golf became an American tradition overnight.

CULTURAL CONSIDERATIONS

When a game is played by more than twenty-five million of the country's inhabitants, and these people spend more than 1.5 billion dollars annually on the game; when it captures several hours of network television programming a week, and syndicated columns are run in more than 100 of the country's leading newspapers; then that game indeed has a great effect on the culture. In addition, golf is of particular interest from a cultural standpoint because it has nurtured an American institution called the *country club* which has now spread worldwide.

Not all golfers are country club members—far from it. Although more than 40 percent of the nation's courses are private, there are five times as many players who participate on public daily-fee courses. Many of the private club players were spawned on public courses, where they developed their interest in golf to the point where club membership was then desired. For a family that wishes to play frequently, joining a reasonably priced club is sometimes a financial necessity.

In some communities, the country club is a gathering place for families from differing economic strata. In other instances it caters exclusively to the ultra-rich, and does not encourage family participation. Clubs determine membership in a variety of ways, this being by social class, financial status, ethnic group, geographical location, religion, or place of business. Some country clubs represent the hedonistic, self-centered, prejudiced, bigoted aspects of our culture; others represent the genuinely healthy atmosphere of sport, family activity, fellowship, and fun, which might just be called a part of the "good life." In either case the country club, primarily due to the sport of golf itself, has become a viable institution in our culture.

MENTAL ATTITUDE

If your approach to the game is to have fun, then you will have to learn occasionally to adopt a philosophical attitude toward your results. You won't *always* play well. One of the attractive qualities of golf, however, is that you don't have to be a great player to enjoy it. You will soon discover that the average player with the right attitude has as much fun, or more, from his kind of game than does a highly skilled individual. The thrill that comes from breaking 100 for the first time is just as great for the amateur as is shooting a round below par for the expert. But don't think the experts don't have some fun too. (Figure 2–1)

You may become one of those rare people who learns to play the game near par, and you can derive much enjoyment from that accomplishment. But if you don't win the club championship or become the best player in your office or school, or even in your weekly foursome, don't despair. Though you may not capture headlines, look at it positively. You will get more shots for your money, exercise more, and see more scenic country than your friends who play the low-scoring, long-hitting game down the middle. In the words of an early golfer:

> If the pleasure of golf lies in hitting the ball,
>   And in seven a hole you do,
> Then I, who have played fourteen in all,
>   Have had twice as much fun as you. (Sutphen 1901, p. 106)

That's the philosophical approach. But to be quite honest with you, the most fun in the game comes when you are improving.

THE CHALLENGE

No one can truly ever say that he has mastered the game of golf. Even the greatest players have been humbled by the game on many occasions. True, some phenomenal rounds of golf have been played in the game's history, but a "perfect round" has yet to have taken place.

At times you will feel that you have mastered your swing or some particular shot, and you may have—temporarily. But if you could collect ten cents for every time a golfer has said, "I finally figured it out; now I have it!" you would be very rich indeed. This *occasional* success is what makes the game a great challenge, for everyone can hit a shot like a professional—*sometimes*. Bobby Jones, perhaps the finest amateur player who ever lived, winner of the U.S. Open, U.S. Amateur, British Open, and British Amateur all in the same year (1930), succumbed to that feeling on at least one occasion. When still a youngster he came bolting into his father's study one day after having shot a 68 on the tough East Lake Country Club golf course, and announced that he never would shoot over 74 again. The following day he shot an 82! A diehard golfer lives on hope—hope for a better tomorrow—knowing full well that he can play better than he did yesterday. There will always be the shot that shouldn't have strayed or the putt that could have been dropped. Herein lies a player's elemental fascination with the game.

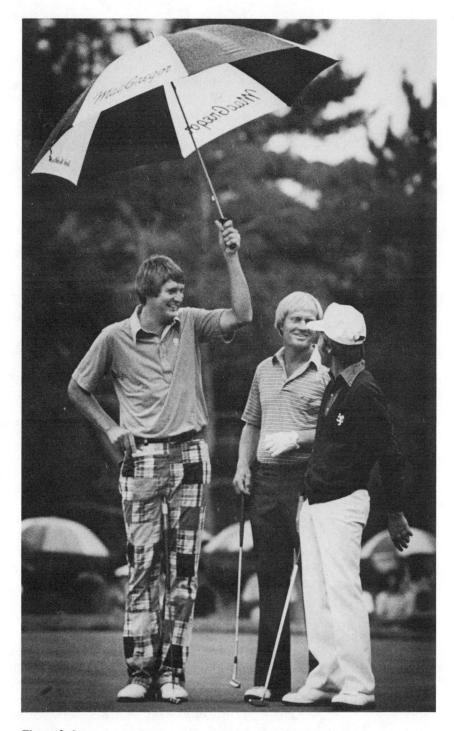

Figure 2–1
Even the stars who play for a living, such as Andy North, Jack
Nicklaus, and Gary Player, find the companionship in the game great fun.

The essentials of golf are quite simple. You need only advance a small ball (1.68 inches in diameter) toward (and eventually, into) a hole four and one-quarter inches in diameter, attempting to do so in the least possible number of strokes. You will have a variety of tools (clubs) with which to accomplish this feat. Between the tee and the cup, however, a great deal can happen. The primary reason that there are unplanned and unwanted occurrences during a round can be attributed to the nature of the facility on which you play—the golf course.

THE COURSE

It is much easier to describe a tennis court, bowling alley, football field, or running track than it is a golf course, since with the exception of minor variations in materials and preparation, the former facilities are standardized. Golf courses have no standardized layout. No two courses in the world truly play alike. The variety in playing facilities is staggering. Adding to the challenges to one's imagination and skill is the factor of weather, which can markedly alter the playing conditions of a course in a matter of minutes. The better courses are carefully designed by a professional golf course architect who tries to shape the natural materials into an attractive and challenging test. Such a course is usually composed of the elements listed in Figure 2-2.

Some courses eliminate sand traps and rough in order to speed up play. Others seek to penalize the least errant shot severely by employing an abundance of traps, water hazards, and trees. (Figure 2-3 A, B, C) Like famous restaurants or unusual natural geographical sites, certain courses develop worldwide acclaim that brings people to test and enjoy their unique contributions to the game. Names like Pine Valley, Pebble Beach, Augusta National, Muirfield, Winged Foot, Merion, and the "mecca," St. Andrews, excite the avid golfer's imagination.

You will be impressed by the game's scenic beauty. Golf courses are located in some of the world's most beautiful settings. In places like Banff, the Monterey Peninsula, Hawaii, Hilton Head, and countless other breathtaking spots, you can be exposed to beauty that provides an aesthetic experience unsurpassed in other sports. (Figure 2-4)

THE SCORECARD

A golf scorecard (Figure 2-5) will be made available to you at the course when you go out to play. It contains basic information about the course and any local rules or conditions that you should know. Local rules will pertain to that particular course only; for example, on a certain course in Florida, you are not required to play your ball when it comes to rest dangerously near an alligator! This type of information is usually located on the back of the scorecard, possibly with a map of the course. On the inside of the card you

Hole—a dogleg to the right
1. Teeing area with 3 sets of markers
2. Paved cart path adjacent to tee and green
3. Fairway—closely mowed grass
4. Rough—long grass, trees, bushes
5. Fairway sand traps or bunkers
6. Special marker trees, bushes, or stakes
   designating 150 yds. to the center of the green
7. Out-of-bounds stakes—usually painted white
8. (a) Water hazard marked by yellow stakes
8. (b) Lateral water hazard marked by red stakes
9. Green-side sand traps or bunkers
10. Putting green and flagstick

HOLE	TEE	YARDAGE	PAR
7	Red	357	4
7	White	407	4
7	Blue	425	4

Figure 2-2

The elements of a golf hole.

13

Figure 2–3A,B,C
The challenges of the game can test the skills of even the finest players.

will find the distance in yards from each set of tee markers to the middle of the green. On some cards, an illustration of the hole is provided, along with distances from easily identifiable landmarks.

Most holes run from just over 100 yards in length to just under 600 yards, with an occasional exception on either end. In addition to the standard-length eighteen-hole course of 6,000 to 7,000 yards there are courses under

Figure 2-4
The prospect of playing one of the fabled courses like Pebble Beach
can quicken the heart of any avid golfer.

6,000 yards, known as *executive courses*, and those even shorter called *par 3 courses*. Par 3 courses have short holes (usually under 250 yards) and are recommended for beginning players. *Par*, a term meaning *the standard of excellence on a given hole*, is based primarily on length (Table 2–1) and is indicative of the average score that an outstanding player would shoot on that hole with errorless play and two putts. The figures in Table 2–1 represent recommendations only, the final determination of par being a prerogative of the local course.

You will also notice a column for handicap on the card. In order to "equalize" players of differing abilities, a national system of *handicapping* has been established by the U.S. Golf Association (USGA). The system is based on the average of a fixed number of a player's best scores. It also takes into consideration the difficulty of the course upon which each score was made. The course's difficulty is expressed by its rating. A player who averages around 80 on a difficult course would probably have a handicap of 6, while a 2 handicapper would average about 75 or 76 strokes per round. If these two people were to compete in match play (a type of competition that determines a winner by the most number of holes won rather than the lowest total score), the 6 handicapper would receive 4 strokes. The handicap figure on the card indicates *where* the player receives them. In this case (using the card in Figure 2–5), it would be on holes 5, 7, 14, and 18, the four most difficult holes. In a women's match with a difference of four in the handicaps, the strokes would fall on 7, 8, 13, and 16.

MEMBER CLUB U.S.G.A. REPLACE DIVOTS / REPAIR BALL MARKS COURSE RATING: RED 68.0 WHITE 69.2 BLUE 70.8

HOLE	1	2	3	4	5	6	7	8	9	OUT	10	11	12	13	14	15	16	17	18	IN	TOTAL	HDCP	NET SCORE
CHAMPIONSHIP BLUE TEES	427	360	140	428	221	362	425	488	351	3187	363	403	187	543	423	183	385	512	434	3433	6635		
WHITE TEES	416	347	135	406	215	349	407	470	346	3062	351	396	176	533	403	175	375	502	422	3333	6414		
PAR	4	4	3	4	3	4	4	5	4	35	4	4	3	5	4	3	4	5	4	36	71		
HDCP	5	13	17	7	3	11	1	15	9		18	6	12	10	2	16	8	14	4				
WON +																							
LOST −																							
HALVED o																							
RED TEES	402	276	121	390	160	339	357	455	346	2818	351	396	166	425	316	117	375	435	339	2913	5765		
LADIES PAR	5	4	3	5	3	4	4	5	4	37	4	5	3	5	4	3	4	5	4	37	74		
LADIES HDCP	7	15	17	5	13	9	3	1	11		14	6	12	2	10	18	4	8	16				

DATE _____ SCORER _____ ATTEST _____

Figure 2–5

A golf scorecard.

Table 2–1   Recommended Determination of Par

PAR	MEN	WOMEN
3	up to 250 yards	up to 210 yards
4	251 to 470	211 to 400
5	471 and over	401 to 575
6		576 and over

THE CLUBS

Golf clubs are simply tools of differing designs that are used to accomplish the task set before the player—to move the ball from one place to another. They are composed of a grip, a shaft, and a head, and are varied to solve two problems most common to the golfer: achieving the proper distance, and the right direction.

A typical golf club is shown in Figure 2–6. Wood clubs, for example, are used for long distances. Because of their length, they can produce greater mechanical force than other clubs. A standard-length driver for men is forty-three inches; for women, forty-two inches. The men's driver is four inches longer than the standard-length 2 iron. This added length makes the driver capable of moving the ball forty to fifty yards farther than the 2 iron for the medium-length-driving player. The shorter irons are for accuracy,

Figure 2–6
The parts of a golf club.

to be used when one is close enough to reach the green. Their greater loft capacity helps the player control distance in that it produces a high trajectory and more backspin that causes the ball to stop soon after landing on the green.

The putter is an almost straight-faced club that is designed to roll the ball, rather than loft it, on the green. Putters come in a variety of styles; therefore, the only way to intelligently select one is to try out several and see what kind of success you have. It is not necessary to have the full complement of irons and woods (fourteen total, including the putter) to play the game.

AFTER READING THIS CHAPTER YOU SHOULD KNOW THAT:

Golf as we know it became popular as early as the 1400s in Scotland but wasn't an established sport in this country until the late 1800s.

The sport of golf has since attained a high degree of popularity and influence worldwide and has been largely responsible for the origin and perpetuation of the country club.

Each golf course is a unique sport facility designed to present the golfer with specific challenges, and has a character all its own.

A scorecard contains information about local rules, par, yardage, course layout, and handicap stroke allocation. This information is helpful in informal play and essential in tournament competition.

Clubs are tools with which to play the game. They have gradual modifications in length and loft, and afford a player a complete range of potential trajectories and distances.

3

EQUIPMENT

ideas on getting started

We will now explore:
1. *What equipment is needed to play the game.*
2. *Whether to rent or buy, and how much to pay for equipment.*
3. *What brands and sizes are best.*
4. *What accessories are needed.*
5. *How to care for your equipment once it is purchased.*

The equipment you use to play golf can have an important effect on the degree of success that you achieve. Good equipment does not make a good golfer, but poor-quality or ill-fitting equipment can certainly hinder the performance of a player at any level of ability.

CLUBS

Rent or Purchase?

If you wish to play and do not own clubs, you may rent them for a nominal fee at almost any golf course pro shop. Rental equipment will suffice until you find out how serious you are about taking up the game. There are, however, several advantages to owning your own clubs. Each set has a particular feel to which you must become accustomed. Owning your own clubs will provide you with the tools for practice and improvement. Having to rent or borrow equipment usually discourages one from regular play.

Where to Buy

Golf equipment is sold in a variety of stores as well as through catalogs, but usually the best place to purchase your equipment is where you play, at your home course golf shop. At a golf shop you have the important advantage of being fit with equipment and should also be able to try it out on the practice range before you buy it. Golf shops will normally stand behind their merchandise 100 percent and will replace faulty equipment within a reasonable length of time after the purchase. Because they expect you to be a regular customer at their place of business, the golf course, they want you to have equipment with which you are satisfied.

What to Pay

Purchasing golf clubs need not be an expensive proposition. Although a full set of top-grade new clubs can run more than your budget may presently allow, there are less costly alternatives. One is a popular combination of clubs called a *starter set* consisting of 1 and 3 woods, 3, 5, 7, and 9 irons, and a putter. The price for a set of clubs of this kind—including a little bag to go with them—is modest compared to that for a full set. As you play more frequently, your judgment of distance will improve rapidly and you will soon find the need for additional clubs. Then it is wise to purchase a higher quality set rather than to add to those clubs you already own.

You may feel that as a new golfer you cannot judge between good quality and lesser quality clubs. However, a difference in performance and feel definitely exists. The discrepancy between top-grade and lower-priced clubs might be described by saying that quality clubs are engineered while inferior ones are "put together." There is painstaking care that goes into designing a top-grade club. Better materials are used, and higher quality control standards are implemented. The very cheapest sets are seldom good buys from either a performance or a durability standpoint. It is well worth the price to pay a few dollars more and invest in at least some degree of quality.

Often your best dollar value can be found in used top-grade equipment. Pro shops also have occasional close-out sales on new equipment at which they offer the previous year's top clubs at good discounts.

What Brands?

Particular brands are hard to recommend because the quality varies in different price categories. The best golf equipment offered today is usually made by one of the following manufacturers: Tommy Armour Golf Company, Spalding, MacGregor, Taylor Made, Titleist, Wilson, Ping, Hogan, Cobra, Northwestern, Powerbilt, Mizuno, Dunlop, and Ram. I don't generally recommend equipment specially made by or for wholesale houses, trading stamp concerns, or department store chains. Although there are exceptions, much of this equipment is of an inferior quality, and the training of the sales staff does not match that of the golf shop professional.

FIT

An experienced player will consider several factors when choosing his or her equipment: the club's length, its shaft flexibility or "whippiness," the swing-weight or balance, grip size and material, head design, lie, and loft. The majority of players can find a proper fit in stock merchandise that does not require special manufacturing. If not, merchandise can be ordered from the factory and received in a matter of weeks. At some golf shops the professional may have his own club-making service. Companies will usually offer merchandise with specialized features, such as shafts which are "extra stiff" for the longest hitting players, as well as "stiff," and "regular" shafts etc., for other players. You may usually choose between rubber, cord, or leather grips in either undersized, oversized, or standard circumferences. *Swingweight*, which is *a measure relating the weight of the clubhead to the weight of the shaft and grip*, traditionally ranges from C0 to C9 for women and from D0 to D6 for men. The higher swingweight numbers and letters represent a heavier-head feeling. In recent years, there has been a trend toward lighter clubs. Large golf manufacturing companies may offer several different designs or models from which to choose. They offer standard lofts and lies for their woods and irons, and custom specifications can also be ordered. Metal woods and perimeter-weighted investment cast irons now dominate the market as they are more forgiving of mishits in their design. Graphite shafts are also rivalling steel for popularity in the marketplace.

Starter sets are made to fit the average player; that is, the clubs have a medium shaft, a regular length and grip size, and are standard in all other dimensions. For a beginner or an infrequent player, these skeleton sets are usually adequate. If, however, you are among that group of people whose body type or level of strength differs markedly from the average, you might want to consider special-order clubs.

Here is one last bit of advice on club buying: Clubs are the single most important equipment item that you will purchase in golf. Poor selection can severely hamper your enjoyment of the game. Get professional advice when you are contemplating the purchase of clubs; a top-priced set given to you as a gift is no bargain if it prevents you from playing well.

OTHER EQUIPMENT

Shoes

The power golf car notwithstanding, golf remains a walking game. If walking makes you uncomfortable, this can certainly lessen your enjoyment of the activity. Therefore, shoes become a vitally important piece of your equipment. Not only do they affect your comfort, but they also play an extremely important role in contributing to the effectiveness of your swing. You can play the game without golf shoes; however, you will find it considerably more difficult, if not impossible, to obtain a solid base from which to swing.

For the majority of conditions in which you will play, a good pair of leather golf shoes that are properly maintained will prove to be the most comfortable and longest lasting of any golf shoes currently on the market. However, shoes made of synthetic materials are less expensive and will certainly suffice in the beginning. Waterproof shoes or golf rubbers are important to have in a wet climate or if you are an all-weather golfer. When purchasing shoes, expect to "get what you pay for" in quality. Good shoes cost more money, but are worth it.

Golf Bags

The type of golf bag you select will, first of all, depend on whether you carry your clubs, ride a golf car, or use a golf pull-cart. In some instances it is easier to carry your bag than it is to pull a cart, particularly when a course is extremely hilly. Carts can be cumbersome to get in and out of your car.

The lightest bags a golfer can carry, called *Sunday bags*, are usually made of nylon, cordura, or vinyl. These bags are highly serviceable and have extra compartments for storing golf accessories.

By the time you are a proficient enough golfer to own a full set of top-grade clubs, you might consider having two golf bags. One should be a large, durable bag with plenty of pockets for sweaters, rain gear, shoes, hand-warmers, golf gloves, tees, balls, ball markers, and an umbrella slip, and the other a light carry bag. The large bag will probably be too heavy to carry around the course comfortably, but can be used with a pull-cart, battery powered cart, or golf car. This handy bag can be used to pack golfing equipment when you travel. (Figure 3–1)

Balls

You will find a wide variety of golf balls from which to choose when you are ready to buy. There are currently three types of construction used in making balls: the conventional three piece ball is made by winding bands of rubber around a core and placing a cover over the sphere; a two-piece or three-piece ball has synthetic material replacing the rubber bands; and a one-piece solid ball is made by injecting the ball's material into a preformed mold. Ironically, the wound ball initially replaced the solid ball on the market in 1902 because it would go much farther. However, over the last two decades the introduction of new synthetics has made it possible to make a solid ball that approximates the wound ball in performance. Since the solid ball is much simpler and less costly to make, it appears inevitable that history will reverse itself.

Figure 3–1
Get a nice light carry bag (such as the one I'm holding in the air) if you want to enjoy walking your round of golf. My Tommy Armour staff bag is for tournament play and exhibitions where I have a caddy, golf car, or cart.

Both solid two piece and wound balls are made in varying compressions or degrees of hardness. Compression ratings range normally from 80 to 100, the higher figure representing the harder ball. Previously, it was thought that it took a very strong person who was a hard swinger to effectively compress a ball rated at 100. It was recommended that a golfer of average length off the tee use a 90 compression ball, and a lighter swinger a ball in the 80 bracket. This theory has been challenged by research teams who contend that the high-compression ball will travel farther for all levels of players. This may be true; however an important consideration is feel, and the higher-compression ball generally feels too hard for the lighter-swinging player.

ACCESSORIES

Carts and Cars

Two types of club-conveying equipment are now in use: the pull cart (both conventional and power assisted) and the riding power golf car. If you do not own a light carry bag and find it difficult to carry your clubs for a full round, then a pull-cart may be a necessary item for you. A good cart can be purchased in a wide range of prices, depending on what accessories are included on it. Inexpensive carts are not very durable and are harder to pull than are the more expensive models. Pull carts may be rented at most public courses.

Electric and gasoline-powered golf cars have been a welcome addition to golf courses for the thousands of people who could not otherwise play. The presence of the powered car has brought many players back to the game who were forced to discontinue play because of physical infirmity. It has also induced many people to play golf who are unable to participate in other sports.

Unfortunately, however, powered golf cars are also being used by normal, healthy individuals who are sorely in need of exercise. An increasing number of courses, anxious for additional revenues, are requiring that everyone who plays the course must use a golf car. At fifteen to twenty-five dollars per round rental, it is easy to comprehend their financial gain. This practice is definitely not in the best interests of the golfer who is being deprived of one of the game's most worthwhile attributes—its exercise value. Don't take "the walk" out of golf; never ride when you can walk.

Gloves

A golf glove assists the player in gripping the club firmly, and also protects the hand from blistering. You may purchase either a full-fingered or a half-fingered glove. The full-fingered model that fits snugly is recommended. The average priced-glove, depending upon the quality of the leather, costs only a bit more than the price of a visor or golf cap, and is a good investment.

Additional Items

1. When buying rainwear, be sure you are purchasing *waterproof* rather than rain-resistant or water-repellent equipment.

2. Tees come in different lengths. If you wish to have extra long tees, ask at the pro shop counter.

3. A *telescoping ball retriever* used for recovering balls from water hazards can pay for itself in a season if the course you play has several such hazards.

4. Golf clothing, as contrasted to street clothing, is specially designed for freedom of movement and comfort while playing.

5. Be cautious about the purchase of golf gimmicks or training systems that offer miraculous results. Some *are* helpful, but get advice from your professional before buying.

MAINTENANCE TIPS

Protect your wood clubs by purchasing a set of head covers. Remove the covers during storage if they get wet. Clean your irons with soap and water, using a bristle brush. Never use abrasive cleaners or cleaning implements that might scratch a chrome finish. Take your rain gear out of the bag after use to prevent mildew. Store your golf glove after each use in a plastic sack that you carry in your bag to keep the leather from drying and hardening. Put a few drops of lubricating oil in the cleat housing of your golf spikes at the time of purchase, and each time you replace the cleats. Wax your wood clubheads occasionally with furniture wax; metal woods can be polished. Leather grips may be washed to maintain their "tackiness." Avoid the use of solvents.

AFTER READING THIS CHAPTER YOU SHOULD KNOW THAT:

Having your own golf clubs is an advantage because it will encourage you to play more frequently and gives you a consistent "feel" one outing to the next.

A starter set, or half set, consists of the odd-numbered clubs in the bag plus the putter, and is a sufficient selection at the beginning.

The majority of players can be "fit" with clubs from standard stock items. If you can't, then consider grip size, shaft length and flexibility, weight, materials in the grip, shaft, and head, and design, loft, and lie when ordering.

Because golf is primarily a walking game, spiked golf shoes are an important item to consider when selecting equipment.

Higher-compression or harder balls will travel farther for all golfers, but may not be practical for some players because of feel.

A golf glove will both protect your hand and give you a better gripping surface.

4

GRIP, AIM, AND SET-UP_____

the preliminaries to the swing

As you prepare to make the swing, you will learn the importance of:
1. Aiming the clubface.
2. Different styles of gripping the club.
3. Body posture, alignment, and ball position.

Having become acquainted with the game of golf and its equipment in the first few chapters, you must now investigate the mechanics needed to develop a sound technique and style of play.

There are two distinct phases to making a successful golf shot. The first phase is somewhat passive, involving your preparations to swing; it will be discussed in this chapter. The second phase is active, and involves performing the swing itself and striking the ball. This more dynamic phase will be dealt with in Chapters 5 and 6.

BEFORE YOU SWING

The fundamental preparations that go into making a good golf shot before the swing could well be labeled the "unappreciated necessities." Just as viewing a successful rocket launch is much more exciting than studying the detailed plans that put the capsule into space, so *swinging,* rather than *preparing to swing,* seems to capture the interest of the amateur golfer. Though the blast-off, or swing, may be sound, without proper preliminaries the result could be unsuccessful. *A golf stroke has a better chance of succeeding with good preparations and a mediocre swing than it does with inadequate preliminaries and a sound swing.*

POSITIONING THE HANDS—THE "GRIP"

Probably the most important aspect of any successfully run operation is its *communications system*. When communication stops, is faulty, or inaccurate, look for problems. The only communication "link" that you have with the golf club is your hands. Proper hand positioning then, becomes a vital key in the process of making a golf shot. This is referred to in most golf circles as *taking your grip*, or just *gripping*. Many people mistakenly interpret that term as "squeezing," the kind of squeezing you see applied to grip strength machines in penny arcades. You don't want to hold a golf club with that type of grip. When we refer to a grip, think more of positioning the hands than of squeezing the club.

It is extremely important to develop a good grip immediately so that your line of communications is correctly established. Find and "set" a fundamentally sound position from the beginning, and stick with it!

The Left Hand

Take a 7 iron at chest height and hold the shaft in the fingers of your right hand angeled toward the right side of your face so that the leading edge of the clubhead is square (pointing vertically to the sky). (Figure 4-1) Now reach out with your left hand in a very natural way and grasp the club in both

Figure 4-1

Figure 4-2

the fingers and palm where you feel you have the most secure pressure with the last three fingers. (Figure 4–2) Position your left hand so that the thumb falls slightly on the right side of the shaft (as though at one o'clock on a clockface), so that you can see three knuckles on the back of your left hand. (Figure 4–3) Notice that the webbing between your thumb and index finger will make a "V" which points between your chin and right shoulder. When you lower the club toward the ground you should feel control in your last three fingers and pressure against the heel pad of your hand. To check and see if you have the correct positioning, let go with your thumb and index finger and waggle the club gently up and down (Figure 4–4). If there is no

Figure 4-3

Figure 4-4

slipping or loss of control you should be okay. Since these three fingers are your primary controllers of the club, it is imperative that you get this portion of the grip correct. In order to find this same position with the club soled, you need to cock your left wrist downward when taking the grip. (Figure 4-5)

The Right Hand

Now hold the club up in front of you again, this time with the correct left hand grip. Make a channel with the fingers of your right hand (Figure 4-6) and starting on the shaft as before, slide it down onto the grip until your right hand contacts the left. (Figure 4-7) Now close your right hand so the thumb falls on the grip at the eleven o'clock position and the "V" formed between your right index finger and thumb points again to a position between your chin and right shoulder. (Figure 4-8) The grip of the right hand

Figure 4-5

Figure 4-6

Figure 4-7

30

Figure 4-8

should feel as though controlled entirely by the fingers. (Think of holding it like a pencil rather than a hammer.) (Figure 4-9) Remember that the left hand control, however, should be felt more in the palm and fingers than simply through the fingers alone.

You now have what is known as a *ten-finger grip* (sometimes erroneously called a "baseball grip"). In other words, all fingers including the two thumbs are in contact with the club (Figure 4-10). Although some successful touring professionals use this method, it is not the grip practiced by 90 percent of the best players throughout the world. There is one more step to perform before you assume the most popular grip position. Extend the little finger of your right hand so that it is removed from the club (Figure

Figure 4-9

Figure 4–10

When you close your left hand you will feel the club securely held by the last three fingers of your left hand.

4–11), then fill that space by sliding your right hand down against the left. The little finger should now lay in the space between the index finger and middle finger of the left. This is the *overlapping grip* (Figure 4–12). What you decide on with regard to final hand position, however, should be a choice made by both you and your instructor relative to your own physical traits.

Figure 4–11

Figure 4–12

Three Types of Grips

There are three basic grip styles: *overlapping, interlocking,* and *ten-finger.* The overlapping grip, named from the great English champion of the early 1900s, Harry Vardon, who popularized the technique, has won the widest acceptance of each of the golf grips by far. But individual differences dictate that one grip may not be the answer for everyone. The goal of sound hand positioning is to provide a balance of power between the two hands while maintaining control and feel. In right-handed players, the dominant right is usually much stronger. To balance the strengths of the two hands and also to produce a better coupling, the overlapping and interlocking positions were devised. Look at the illustrations and descriptions of the styles in Figure 4–13 and check the accompanying chart to help you decide which method suits you. Some experimentation may be necessary, but with the help of a teacher or professional, you should initially settle on one method and stick with it.

Closed or open position.   This involves getting the "Vs" correct. It would be foolish to assume that everyone should grip a club in exactly the same way. This is both impossible and impractical—impossible because hands come in a great variety of sizes and shapes, and impractical because hands vary in strength and flexibility.

Description of Three Grip Styles
(Club held vertically with the clubhead in the air)

Overlapping	Interlocking	Ten Finger
Slide your right hand down the grip until your little finger rests in the notch made by the middle finger and the slightly triggered index finger of your left hand. Your little finger does not have to hook clear around the knuckle.	Remove the index finger of your left hand and, moving your right hand slightly down the grip, lace the two fingers together. Maintain your right-hand grip primarily in the fingers.	Explained in the text. All fingers and two thumbs on the grip.

Criteria for Selection

	Overlapping	Interlocking	Ten Finger
FINGER AND HAND SIZE...	Normal to large	Small hands, thick fingers	Usually smaller hands
STRENGTH...	Normal to strong	Normal to strong	Usually weaker
HAND BALANCE...	Strong right dominance	Right dominance	Less dominant right
EST. % OF USE*...	63%	25%	10%

* Approximately 2% use some other grip.

Figure 4–13

Descriptions of Three Grip Placement Styles (Club held vertically with the clubhead in the air)

The "Vs" formed between the thumb and index finger of each hand, or the number of knuckles visible on top of the hands, can provide a reference for consistent and correct hand positioning. These "Vs" should point somewhere between your chin and right shoulder. Exactly where will be determined in large part by your strength. Players with stronger arms and hands and commensurate flexibility favor a position more toward the chin. Those weaker or less flexible players prefer the "Vs" pointing more toward their right shoulder. Improper positioning will tend to produce the type of results shown in the last two illustrations of Figure 4–14.

The exact number of knuckles that will show and the place where the "Vs" from the web between the thumbs and index fingers point are two mechanics to be decided on finally after you have hit a few balls. The most

ADDRESS POSITIONS

Normal
Grip
Position

Closed Face*
Grip
Position

Open Face**
Grip
Position

PROABLE IMPACT POSITIONS

Square Face   Closed Face   Open Face

* Formerly called strong grip.
** Formerly called weak grip.

Figure 4-14
Three grip positions and their influence on the clubface at impact.

natural and sensible position is one in which your arms are hanging comfortably, and you need only to swing into a position where your fingers may encircle the grip. But slight adjustments may be necessary and can be found through some experimentation. Apply the fundamentals that you have learned about gripping, and then adjust the position of your hands until you can hit the ball straight. You will probably find the correct position will be very close to your normal arm hang grip. (Figure 4-15)

Figure 4-15

Grip Pressure

How much grip pressure do you exert to position your hands properly? We sometimes hear the words "firmly" and "lightly" used in reference to grip, but these terms are only relative. What is firm to a person with weak hands may be light to another with stronger hands. The best way to test for the correct amount of grip pressure is to ask these questions:

Too firmly?

Is the blood being squeezed from my fingers?
Are my forearms tight?
Do I have little wrist suppleness?
Am I unable to sense the weight of the clubhead when I swing?
When swung does the club feel like a long stiff stick?
If the answer to any of these questions is "yes," you are probably gripping the club too tightly, most likely in the right hand.

Too lightly?

Does the club turn in my left hand when I hit the ball?
Is there daylight showing between my fingers and the grip?
Does the club bounce at the top of my backswing?
Is there a hole or space formed at the base of my left little finger, which comes from not having my little finger securely encircling the grip?
If you can answer "yes" to any of these questions, you are probably gripping too loosely, most likely in your left hand.

Take great care in developing your grip, and frequently consult with your teacher about your progress. Above all, be patient and particular. A good grip is an invaluable asset to your development as a golfer. Now check Figures 4–16 to 4–18 to make sure you are proceeding correctly.

Once you have determined the grip you plan to use you must learn to aim or align the clubface and your body to see that you are "set up" correctly in relation to the ball. Golf is a target game which uses a ball as an object with which to hit a specific target. If you want to drive a ball in any sport toward a given spot, you must present the striking surface of your bat, club, paddle, hand, etc. at right angles to your intended line of flight.

Figure 4-16

In golf the striking surface is the clubface. If your ball rebounds to the right of your target, the face has been presented "open" (in golf terminology); if the ball goes to the left, it has come in "closed." To learn to hit the ball straight consistently, you must be able to swing your clubhead on a path toward the target and return the face squarely to the ball repeatedly. You can check to see that you start the clubface in that position and also find the proper "set-up" by using the following simple exercise.

Figure 4-17

Figure 4–18

Using three clubs, make a simulated letter "H" as illustrated in Figure 4–19. Club A will point to the target and is called the *target line*. Club B represents the *foot line* on which the toes of each foot will be placed when assuming a square stance. Club C, which is at right angles to the others, is called the *ball line* and indicates the position of the ball relative to your feet. Ball position is an important part of this set-up. Now stand comfortably so that your toes are almost parallel to the foot line and turned slightly out, as in Figure 4–20. Take your grip with a 5 or 7 iron, and sole the club on your target line. When the leading edge of your iron makes a right angle to line A, you are soling the club with a squared face. Let the grip end of your club point to your left hip when practicing this exercise. Spend some time in your first few practice sessions checking this so that you become accustomed to seeing the correct club positioning. This is important, for when you actually play, the ball will rest in the grass and no artificial alignment devices will be allowed. You may also check your body alignment by setting a club across your shoulders (Figure 4–21) and hips. (Figure 4–22)

There is an athletic, at-ready position known as *stance* that is common to many sports, including golf. With only slight changes of body attitude, you will find that shortstops, quarterbacks, defensive basketball players, tennis players, and many other athletes prepare for action by spreading their feet to shoulder width, flexing their knees, and bending slightly forward at the waist. Making these adjustments from the upright carriage position gives the player a solid base from which to move, lowers the center of gravity, and improves equilibrium.

Figure 4-19
Place two clubs parallel on the ground. Point the one farthest from you (A) just to the right of your target so that a similar line running through your ball (T) will point to your target. The closer club—line (B)—is for your foot alignment, helping set your body parallel to the flight line. The third club (C) is to aid in determining ball position.

Figure 4-20

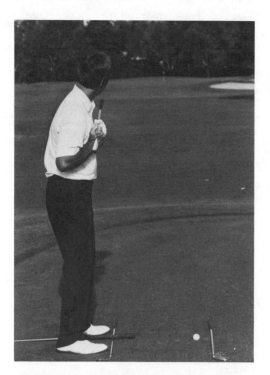

Figure 4–21
Check your shoulder alignment by placing a club across your shoulders. It should be pointing parallel to your target line and to the left of the target.

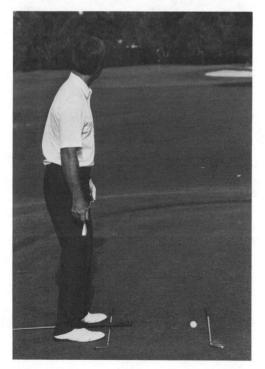

Figure 4–22
To further help you check your body alignment, place a club across your thighs to check hip positioning. It should be parallel to your target line and left of the target.

This position can also be adapted to golf. With both hands placed on the grip—while the shaft is fixed in a continuous line with the left arm—elevate the club in front of you. Gradually bring your arms and the club down until with the arms you feel slight pressure on the chest. (Figure 4–23) Bend forward at the hips to a point where the club is touching the grass (Figure 4–24). Finally, flex your knees slightly, just enough to sole the club properly (Figure 4–25).

This technique will help you determine the correct distance to stand from the ball with all clubs, while taking into consideration your body build. Tall, lean people will end up standing closer to the ball than heavier-set types. But in any case you should feel your arms "hanging" rather than "reaching"—in an extended rather than limp position. The flexing of the knees will give your swing cushioning that will allow you to turn on the power without losing your fluid motion.

Feet and Weight

Finding the correct positioning for your feet and weight is a simple matter; more than likely you will do it intuitively. The feet should be spread to about shoulder width to stabilize balance. Some men seem to have a tendency to spread their feet wider than women ordinarily do, in order to hit the ball harder. Actually, a wide spread often decreases distance since too much space between the feet can inhibit the turning of the hips and shoulders, a move essential to power. Female players will sometimes stand with their feet too

Figure 4–23

Figure 4–24

Figure 4–25

close together and therefore lack adequate balance to wind up and take a full cut.

There are two directions in which one's weight can be balanced: *forward-backward* and *laterally*. You can maintain the best forward-backward balance by distributing weight between the balls and heels of your feet—never on the toes or heels alone. Your lateral balance will vary somewhat depending on the club you are using. The weight at address tends to favor the left side on a short-iron pitch swing (about 60 percent left to 40 percent right), but equalizes more as the stance becomes wider and can even become 60 percent right and 40 percent left when you reach the driver. On all swings the weight that is on the right foot at address should exert some pressure on the inside of that foot, so that the right leg may better resist too much lateral movement to the right and be able to push toward the left during the forward swing.

Your feet should be arranged so that the back foot, while comfortable, points on a line almost at right angles to your target. If you have difficulty in making a backswing of adequate length, turn it farther outward. The left foot will be turned ten to twenty degrees out from this line toward your target. Turning the left foot out will help you clear your left side so that you can complete the hitting action all the way through the shot. If a line were drawn from your right toe through the left toe in your regular stance, it would run parallel to your line of flight; this is known as a *square stance*. The open and closed stances are variations that are used for specific types of shots, since they can influence the line on which you swing and therefore affect the flight of the ball (Figure 4–26).

Ball Placement

Two theories on ball placement are common. One would have you assume a different stance for every club. The other, the one that will be demonstrated here, prefers the ball be in a constant position relative to your left foot on all irons, with only slight changes made for the woods. In the constant-positioning method, the ball for all iron shots is placed between three and four inches toward the center of the stance from a line inside the left heel. The only variable is the right foot, which controls the width of the stance and the center line of your body. The width of your stance will decrease as the shot becomes shorter.

With the wood clubs played from the grass (fairway woods), move the ball one to two inches farther toward your left foot. The driver, since it is hit from a tee, can be played even farther forward. Place it just in back of a line from your left heel or instep. You will acquire slight variations in these positions as you develop your own style of play.

The most important considerations in stance and ball placement are:

1. Stand comfortably, weight favoring your left side more on shorter shots, balanced on medium shots, and favoring the right slightly on tee balls (driver).

Probable swing line related to stance

"On target"

Square
(for straight shot)

Probable swing line related to stance

"Outside-in"

Open
(for slice or roll)

Probable swing line related to stance

"Inside-out"

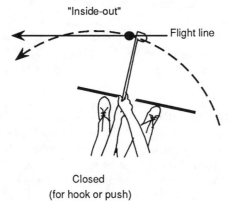

Closed
(for hook or push)

Figure 4–26

Influence of stance alignment on swing path.

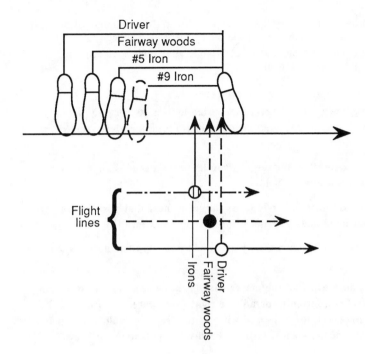

Figure 4-27

Relationship of ball to feet in the stance.

2. Keep the ball placed far enough forward from the middle of your stance so that you don't have to "reach back" to hit it.

3. Stand so you are neither crowding the ball nor reaching out for it.

Developing a Routine

The more consistent you can become in making these preparations before you swing, the greater your chances for success. Therefore, try to develop a routine that you can follow automatically in the course of getting ready to hit a golf shot.

1. Assess your lie to determine the kind of shot you can hit.

2. Determine your target's distance by judging the wind, weather conditions, and terrain to aid in club selection.

3. Visualize the shot you plan to hit, including the trajectory and final result.

4. Select your club and begin to feel how you intend to swing it.

5. Approach your shot from behind the target line so that you can visualize where you intend to aim.

6. Take your correct grip.

7. With your left arm on your chest, sole the clubhead behind the ball while measuring the correct distance to stand away from the ball. Check to see that the bottom line of the clubface is at a right angle to your line of flight. Place your feet so that they are aligned correctly, and the ball is placed correctly in relation to them.

8. Draw an imaginary line (line of flight) to the target and visualize that line approaching the ball from the inside on your forward swing.

9. Stay comfortable and relaxed while your body is in motion.

10. Make your best swing.

YOUR PRACTICE SHOULD BEGIN WITH THE REALIZATION THAT:

Many golf shots are "spoiled" before the swing ever starts because of faulty preparation. In fact, most swinging errors stem from an incorrect grip, stance, or alignment.

The clubface is "square" to the target when its bottom edge is aligned at right angles to the intended line of flight.

Your hands are positioned squarely to the target or near that position when the back of your left hand and the palm of your right hand face it.

Because of individual differences, all players will not grip the club in exactly the same manner.

A correct golf stance will find the player with his arms in an extended hanging position, with feet comfortably spread, the right knee braced inward, and the weight balanced between the balls and heels of the feet. The ball is placed forward of the center of the stance, farther ahead for woods than for irons.

You should develop a definite routine in your advance preparations to allow you to find the correct grip, aim, and set-up on all your shots consistently.

5

THE GOLF SWING _____

a feeling to be developed

You are now ready to learn how to:
1. Identify the important principles of the swing.
2. Fit them to your abilities and body type.

Golf's greatest players agree that legendary PGA professional Sam Snead had a "classic swing." It was a picture of flowing but powerful rhythm, culminating in a sweep of the club through the ball that excluded the slightest hint of forced effort. It was reminiscent of a perfectly executed swan dive from five meters—never a hurried move, never a loss of control. Contrast that with the lashing swing of Mark Calcavecchia, the laconic lightness of Larry Mize, the mechanical precision of Nick Faldo, and the abbreviated but powerful swat of Dan Pohl—all touring professionals. Then tell me which swing is best. Well, Snead's was best—that is, for Snead. And probably, it would also be the best swing style for most novice golfers to emulate. True, it may not work for Faldo or Mize or the others because they may be physically constructed to swing in another way. You may not be able to swing like Sam Snead either, but chances are that the closer you get to that rhythm and sequence, within your own limitations, the better you will play.

All of the above players have developed a personalized style that has become successful for them only after countless hours of experimentation and practice. For the most part, they swing the golf club quite well, but some of their swinging habits should *not* be copied! Obvious physical differences and limitations will tell you that if you are six feet, five inches, and 175 pounds, or five feet, nine inches, and 200 pounds, you won't be able to swing just like five-foot, nine-inch, 165-pound Tom Kite no matter how hard you try. More subtle discrepancies between you and a PGA tour star may exist in strength, flexibility, and even in temperament, which will dic-

47

tate a necessary difference in style. So as you start your golf swing education, recognize that individual differences among successful players exist. Then consider the following suggestions:

1. Most instructional books written by professionals are "How I Do It" books, or personal testimonies of the techniques that a particular pro uses.

2. Be aware that what works wonders for Nicklaus may not work for you.

3. With so many varied, expert opinions available, select one system and stay with it. Trying to build an effective swing by using a little of the best from several contrasting methods is actually quite difficult, if not impossible.

4. In choosing a player to emulate, select a pro who resembles you in body type and in temperament if possible.

THEORY OF THE SWING

Now that you are aware that certain differences exist in the swings of fine players, let's see in which ways their swings are alike. In searching for similarities, try to discard the mannerisms that needn't be copied, and instead focus your attention on the principles that make their swings work. Any golf swing must have these essentials: *clubhead speed, accuracy,* and *consistency* or repeatability. If any of these three items is lacking, it is virtually impossible to become a good player.

In order to blend these three characteristics into a fine golf swing, the following principles are employed by the best players:

1. The club is swung in a nearly circular fashion around the player, *away from,* then *toward* the target.

2. The center of rotation or hub of that swing is located in the general area of the player's spine.

3. The wrists hinge, providing a second lever in the swing, which generates additional force.

4. As the swing approaches impact, angular momentum travels from the center of the swing out to the clubhead, thereby slowing the arms down and speeding up the clubhead. This force allows the clubface to square itself to the target without the additional manipulation of the hands.

5. The focus should be on *swinging* the club *through* to a balanced finish rather than hitting *at* the ball.

Though these principles mean little to you at the moment because they have not yet been put into effect, it is important to become acquainted with them. As you begin to convert your mental perception of the swing into action, you can come back to them again to see if you are on the right track.

FEELING A SWING

There are two approaches to striking a golf ball—*swinging* and *hitting*. The swinging style is what will be advocated in this book because it follows exactly the principles that we have just discussed. To develop consistency in a hit-emphasis style takes years of practice and the hitting of thousands of practice balls. In addition, it requires strength and a great deal of playing and practicing to learn the timing for successful repetition.

On the other hand, a swinging hit makes less demands on the golf student and does not require as much practice to develop. When we talk of swinging we consider a smooth-flowing action with gradual acceleration that can allow the player to feel centrifugal force through the clubhead.

DEVELOPING A SWING

Footwork

In any striking or throwing motion in which you are trying to generate speed, the transfer of weight and the development of power that comes from trunk rotation are important. To develop these features, you must establish a fundamental known as *footwork*. Your first physical introduction to the golf swing in this book will be to take a part of the swing—the footwork involved— and develop it in conjunction with an arm swing.

Place a club on the ground to represent your target line. Then stand with your feet shoulder width apart, with your arms hanging in front of you. Bend forward at the waist and flex your knees slightly to assume a position similar to your correct golf posture. (Figure 5-1A) Keep your upper arms close to your sides. Now imagine you are a wheel, a large wagon wheel: Your arms are the spokes, and your head is the hub. Start to swing your arms by rotating your trunk and shoulders to the right, letting your arms move in that direction. (Figure 5-1B) Then reverse the direction to the left to unwind the wheel. Your arms will return to their starting position, initiated by a weight shift to the left, then continue over the left shoulder to finish. Gradually increase your turning until your chin meets your left shoulder on the backswing and your right shoulder on the follow-through. This should be done in such a way that your head moves very little during the swing except to rotate slightly to the right on the backswing and to the left and up on the follow-through. The head may also move laterally to the right on longer shots like the drive, but must return to its starting point. Your arms should hang separately and fold slightly at the elbows, hugged a bit to your side during this drill.

Observe the accompanying footwork that results from the correct performance of this winding and unwinding as pictured. On the backswing you will feel a desire to raise your left heel in the air as you complete the full windup of your shoulders and hips. This is correct in a full-motion swing for a long shot. But if the heel is elevated more than a couple of inches, it is a warning sign that indicates that your head is probably moving laterally too far to the right and upward as well. Keep your head more still so that

Figure 5–1A

DRILL 1 ARMS HANGING. Place a club on the ground with the grip pointing to your target. Let your arm hang in front, right hand below left, and align them on the middle of the shaft. As you swing you will see your hands come from inside the club line onto the shaft going toward the grip, then back to the inside again.

Figure 5–1B

Swing your arms back so as to wind your upper body over your right leg. Position your back to face the target. Your left heel may rise slightly and your left knee will flex inward. Don't lift your right arm but rather let it fold by bending at the elbow so that the right arm remains fairly close to your side.

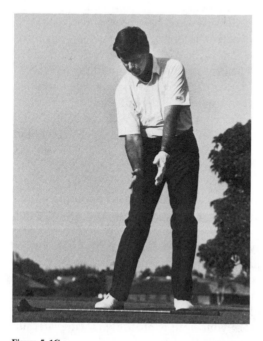

Figure 5–1C

Swing through a position similar to that at address, except that now the weight is more on the left foot and there is a bit more "sit" in your knees. The back of the left hand and right palm face the target in the impact position, mimicking their grip alignment at address. This is critical.

Figure 5–1D

Finish on the left side while comfortably erect with the right heel in the air pointing vertically. Turn to a position directly facing the target if it is physically possible for you to do so.

your arms will rotate around it in a *turning*, not a lifting, action. The heel will then stay closer to the ground.

The most important part of your footwork will come after you have reached the top of your backswing, when the upper half of your body is over your right knee. At that point, reverse the direction of your swing motion by first getting your left heel down on the ground solidly by transferring your weight towards your left leg. This is done in a fashion similar to that of throwing a ball in a side-arm, under-arm fashion. Roll off the inside of your right foot, while your hips move laterally and rotate to the left. Let the palm of your right hand and the back of your left hand face your target at the impact position. (Figure 5-1C) Upon completion of this motion, your belt buckle should make a ninety-degree turn from its original face-the-ball position to one facing the target or beyond. Now your weight will be almost completely on the outside of your left foot. (Figure 5-1D)

You must practice these fundamentals without a club until they become automatic, first with both arms swinging (Drill 1), then with the left arm alone (Drill 2: Figures 5-2A, B, C, and D); then using the left arm with three fingers of the right gripping the left thumb (Drill 3: Figures 5-3A, B, C, D) and continuing through to Figures 5-4, 5-5, 5-6, and 5-7. This series of drills will beautifully prepare you for the next step, which places an object, the ball, in the way of your swing. Unless you have mastered these elementary positions it is a waste of time to try to hit practice balls, let alone play. In several practice sessions of five to ten minutes, you can acquire these necessary basic skills. (Figure 5-8)

When you do these drills pay attention to the following points:

1. Make a full shoulder turn on the backswing so that you literally "wind up" and have your back face the target. (Figure 5-1B)

2. While feeling your upper body weight over your right leg, keep your head reasonably well-centered so that you can learn to return to a position where you can make contact with the ball consistently. (Figure 5-1B)

3. Have your wrists cocked with the back of your hand either flat or arched slightly at the top of the swing. Release the cocking on your downswing so that you hear a "whooshing" sound when swinging the club, as the back of your left hand faces the target at impact. (Figure 5-1B and 5-1C)

4. Practice all swings so that your hands come from the inside down the line, to slightly outside of that line, then back again to the inside of the club placed on the ground. (Figure 5-1C)

5. Always transfer your weight to your left side during the forward swing. (Figure 5-1D)

Getting to the Top of the Backswing

You now have most of the important elements fundamental to a good golf shot: *grip, stance, alignment,* and *footwork.* All that remains is for you to get the club to the top of your swing in the correct plane in a square position, and to deliver it to the ball that way.

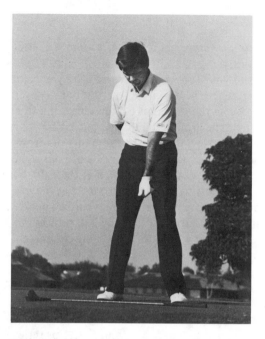

Figure 5–2A

DRILL 2 LEFT ARM ALONE. Make a fist with your left hand and point your extended thumb above the club shaft. Place your right hand behind your back.

Figure 5–2B

Wind to the top of your swing so that the left thumb is parallel to the target line. Keep your left hand closed and wrist flat or only slightly cupped.

Figure 5–2C

The back of the left hand faces the target at impact.

Figure 5–2D

Finish on the left side. Your left hand will still be closed and the thumb will point away from your target. Your left wrist is still flat, or if continuing farther, may cup slightly behind you. Be sure your left arm is folded, as indicated in

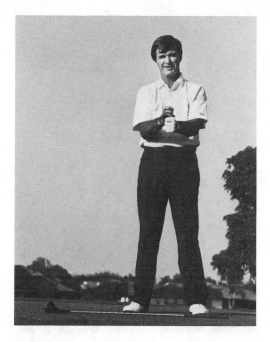

Figure 5–3A

DRILL 3 ADD RIGHT HAND. This is exactly the same as DRILL 2 except that you grip your extended left thumb with the index, middle, and ring fingers of your right hand, while keeping the little finger of the right hand free. At address, your right elbow will relax and point toward your right hip.

Figure 5–3B

Swing to the top, left wrist flat, right side relaxed. Do not lift! Let your hands move over your right shoulder comfortably. Note that the upper body weight is over the right knee.

Figure 5–3C

Shift from the right to left side, returning the back of your left hand square to the target, with the palm of the right hand facing the target and the right elbow near your side.

Figure 5–3D

Same finish as in DRILL 2 except that the right hand now accompanies the left. The right elbow will be relaxed again and point downward rather than to the side.

Figure 5-4A

DRILL 4 CLUB SIDE DOWN. With your left hand grip a wood club by the neck so that the club is upside down. Add your right hand grip lightly, then repeat the positions of the previous drills.

Figure 5-4B

Swing to the top with the left wrist flat or cupped slightly and the left thumb pointing parallel to the target line. The upper body is positioned over the right knee.

Figure 5-4C

Transfer the weight to your left side, and throw your right hand off the club just prior to the impact position to make the back of your left hand face the target at impact.

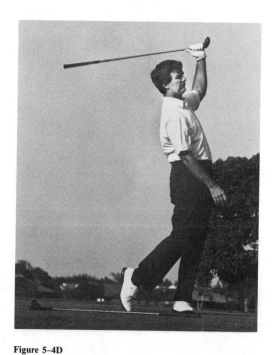

Figure 5-4D

Let your left side continue to its finish. This should make a whooshing sound if you generate sufficient speed. The upper body should now be over the left knee.

Figure 5-5

DRILL 5 LEAVE THE RIGHT HAND ON.
Follow DRILL 4 exactly, but leave the right
hand on the club throughout the swing. Try
not to exert greater right hand grip pressure,
which will slow the speed and decrease the
loudness of the "whoosh."

A very important part of getting the club to the top correctly is found
in the takeaway. For the first couple of feet of your backswing, you should
try to maintain the same relationship between the left arm and clubface that
you had at address. (Figure 5-9) This means keeping the face in a square
position, one that would still be at a right angle to the target if you were
to reverse your direction and return the clubface to the ball. To complete
this maneuver, take the club back by pushing it away with your left arm,
supported and aided by your right hand. When the club passes your right
leg, the arc of the backswing will start upward more noticeably. The wrists
will begin to cock as they near the height of the right hip. The correct wrist
cock is simple, but at first may seem a little awkward or unnatural. To practice it, hold your left arm in front of you at chest level comfortably, with
the fist closed and with thumb extended, pointing upward on line with your
right ear. Take hold of your thumb with the first three fingers of your right
hand as though gripping the club. Now cock your wrist so that your left thumb
inclines straight back toward your right ear. It won't come very far; in fact,
it won't feel like you have cocked it much at all. This could explain the unnatural feeling. What you will see when you do this correctly is a few wrinkles
forming under your thumb. If wrinkles appear also under your wrist, you
have flexed your wrist dorsally (to the left), a position that encourages one
of golf's major errors, the *slice*. An example of the slice is depicted in Figure
5-10A. To guard against that happening, keep your forearm and wrist in
a straight line or reasonably close to it. You may develop that feeling by plac-

Figure 5-6A

DRILL 6 RIGHT HAND COMING OFF 7 IRON. Choke down on your grip for greater control of the now heavier weight in your hand. Swing to the top position you have been practicing. Let your right hand assist in stabilizing the takeaway, thereby completing the backswing and positioning your left wrist correctly. Otherwise let it follow the left arm swing.

Figure 5-6B

Just prior to impact, remove the right hand grip. The back of the left hand should be moving toward the target.

Figure 5-6C

Finish as in previous drills. Make sure that the last three fingers have not opened up and that your left wrist has not collapsed.

Figure 5–7A

DRILL 7 FULL SWING 7 IRON. From a normal grip position swing the club to the top while the position of your arms, hands, and body remain as they have been throughout the previous six drills.

Figure 5–7B

Return impact with weight to the left, with the back of the left hand facing the target.

Figure 5–7C

Finish in a comfortable "face-the-target position, as you did in the other drills. Now put a ball on a tee to practice the swing you have developed.

Figure 5-8

THE FORWARD SWING. A) Address, in balance, relaxed but ready. B)
Takeaway with upper body over right knee, with wrists cocking, and right leg
stable. C) The top of the swing. The right leg is slightly flexed but braced. The left
knee points to a spot just behind the ball when the shoulders have made their full
turn. The left heel can be off the ground slightly. D) The weight shift turn and
pull. The left side begins its lateral move and turn accompanied by a weight shift
rotation of the hips and forward pull of the left arm—a wide radius. The left arm
continues to lead in an extended position as the weight is being transferred to the
left leg. E) Impact. Contact is made with the ball as the right arm extends and the
weight shifts to the left. The head stays back. The hips turn through as the swing
extends toward the target. The left knee is still slightly flexed. F) A strong finish.
Good body motion and footwork will result in the right foot finishing on its toe
with the right knee and stomach pointing toward the target. A strong extension will
bring the hands to a full finish.

Figure 5–9

Keeping the clubface square in the "one-piece takeaway."

ing a book flat on the back of your hand so that it covers the wrist and extends from the knuckles to midforearm. Cock your thumb back as far as
you can, keeping the book either firm and flat or to allow for a small bridge
if you have a three-knuckle grip on the left hand. This is the position your
left hand should be in at the top of your swing. (Figure 5–10B)

The remainder of your backswing will simply be a continuation of
the extended left side–dominated motion that is already underway. The
takeaway and backswing constitute an arm swing that powers the turn of
the shoulders, the trunk, and the hips in a chain fashion. Although dominated
by the left side, the right hand is quite important during the backswing, not
only for what it does but also for what it *doesn't* do. The role of the right
side at this point is to remain passive for the most part, though the grip in
your right hand does stabilize the left in the initial portion of the backswing,
helps in getting the backswing completed, and supports the left arm at the
top of the backswing. A moderately relaxed right grip will allow your right
wrist to cock so that your hand can rest correctly under the shaft at the top
of the swing. With an absence of tension in your right arm at the top of
the swing, the right elbow will point almost toward the ground, a position
that has been likened to that of a waiter carrying a tray. If tension is present
in your right side because you are using your right hand and arm to pick
up the club in the backswing, then your right elbow will fly into the air and
point directly behind and away from you. Finally, the right hand should not
roll the face open or pull the backswing sharply inside on the takeaway.

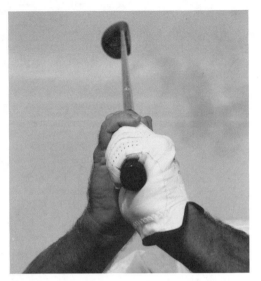

Figure 5–10
Clubface and wrist positions at the top of the backswing.

A

Open clubface at the top of the backswing, left wrist cupped, right elbow flying outward.

B

Square Clubface, left wrist flat, right elbow pointing downward.

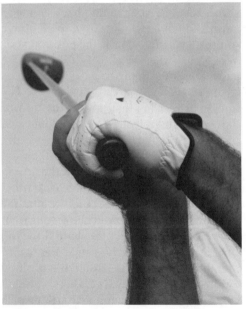

C

Closed Clubface, left wrist bowed, right elbow tighter to the ride side of the body.

Swinging in Plane

One of the principles of swinging noted at the beginning of this chapter was to swing the club close to a single plane. Although this plane does change slightly on the downswing from the one taken on the backswing, at this point consider it as being the same as the backswing. A baseball swing at chest height resembles a horizontal plane; an underhand softball pitch is vertical; and the golf swing falls somewhere in between. Errors result when a swing gets out of plane or "off the track." To find the correct plane, simply imagine that type of spoked wheel (illustrated in Figure 5–11) that is tilted around your body and that points in the direction of your line of flight. To check and see if the club is on that correct plane, grip a driver at the very middle of its shaft. During the backswing and downswing, an extension from the butt end of the grip should point to the intended path when striking the ball.

Return and Impact

If you are in the correct position at the top of the backswing, the rest will be much easier. To make the downswing, all you have to do is transfer your weight to the left while pulling with an extended left arm, and let the clubhead swing through the ball to a full finish—more a feeling than a mechanized motion.

To acquire that feeling you should understand that the movement from the top of the swing to the finish is primarily one of weight shift, uncoiling, and is a pulling rather than a pushing or early casting action. It is

Figure 5–11
The swing plane visualized as extending to the target.

as though you were going to "sling" the club down the fairway. The correct sequence of the action—feet, legs, hips, trunk, arms, and hands—blends the forces and brings them to a summation at impact, the moment of truth. In Figure 5–12, I am practicing this critical position by using an Impact Bag.* Note the left and right hand positions in Figure 5–13.

A most helpful practice exercise, drill 5–6 will make you acutely aware of the uncoiling feeling that comes from transferring your weight to the left and uncoiling your body. Take your proper grip and stance position. Swing your arms and club away so that your shoulders and hips turn to make a full backswing while your left wrist cocked in a square position and your left arm is extended. Start your downswing with a shift of weight, accompanied by the arms starting downward, then a lateral move and turn of the hips toward the target. Feel the muscles in your back and particularly those under your left shoulder, until you approach your right hip or thigh. *Keep your wrists fully cocked to this point.* When it seems as though it is almost too late to get the clubhead through, let it fly, utilizing centrifugal force. To realize that it will catch up to your hands without your help, let go with your right hand (in a practice swing) in the impact zone. There is no way you can stop the club from lashing through! You could retard its speed, however, by adding grip pressure, particularly squeezing with your right hand if it were on the club—which is what the majority of unskilled players do. This experience should demonstrate conclusively to you that you won't *consciously* need to hit with your right hand at all to produce distance. You may, and some players do, but you don't need to. The right hand has a role to play in adding power to the swing, but is best utilized when no concentrated attempt is made to use it for that purpose. Instead, work diligently on strengthening your left side, for the forces generated by the unwinding of your body and the pulling action of your whole left side produce the *swinging hit* that is so characteristic of the centrifugal force powered swing.

A natural release of the energy that has built up in the swing will also help the clubface to square itself to the ball so that your direction will be true. If your energy is correctly released, you will be able to feel the weight of the clubhead, as if it were a rock on the end of a rope. Trying to "hit at" the ball rather than swing the club to target produces tension in your hands that can slow the clubhead down. A correct release will allow the club to complete a full follow-through in a natural manner. A good finish indicates the quality of the action that has gone on before.

There are exceptions to the type swing we have described. One is when a player, for physical reasons, can wind his body only a moderate amount, thus limiting his range of motion. Then he or she must emphasize the use of an active right-hand leverage-type hit.

---

*Impact Bag available from: Golf Around the World
564 Greenway Dr.
N. Palm Beach, FL 33408

Figure 5-12

Here is one of the best practice devices I've ever used. It's called an Impact Bag®. This aid teaches the feel and position of correct impact.

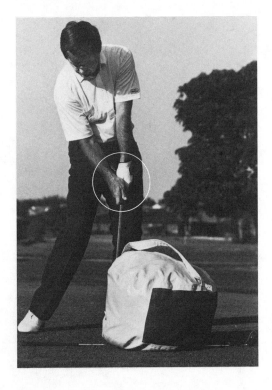

Figure 5-13

Note the position of the back of the left hand. This is how all the great players look at impact when swinging correctly.

THIS CHAPTER HAS SHOWN YOU THAT:

Individual differences may affect the "mannerisms" of your swing, but there are certain principles in swinging that cannot be overlooked.

The golf swing is roughly circular in motion, made close to a single plane with a rotational "center" located at the top of the spine.

When you swing, (as opposed to *hit*) there is a definite feeling of weight at the end of the club that is the result of centrifugal force.

In the swinging hit style, the ball appears to jump off the clubface and travel farther than expected for the effort made.

Good footwork is the foundation on which the swing is built. It should be mastered before a player attempts practicing using balls.

You should be concerned with developing the strength of your left side in order to properly balance the role of your right.*

*Ways to strengthen the left or nondominant side, could include using a grip squeezer to work the left hand; swinging a sand wedge with the left arm alone, hip height to hip height, while playing and carrying the golf bag; doing extra "reps" for the left side while weight training; swing a weighted club and emphasize the left's role.

6

THE FULL SWING APPLIED TO IRONS AND WOODS

the same principles with adjustments

This chapter will tell you how to apply:
1. *The basic swing to both the irons and the woods.*
2. *The adjustments for each of the two types of shots.*
3. *The way to achieve the most consistent distance in your shots.*

Now that you have been introduced to the principles of the swing and the fundamental preparations that precede it, it's time to apply that knowledge to some golf shots. The answers to the following questions should become clear to you as you progress through the chapter. What two words must you keep in mind when first learning to hit an iron shot? Why do some balls that you hit become airborne, while others roll along the ground? What are some of the factors that influence distance, and how are these best applied to the swing?

THE IRONS

Irons are the most versatile clubs in your set because they offer the widest range of trajectory and distance. All irons, however, are designed for one basic purpose: to get the ball onto the green. To do that, you must first learn to get the ball into the air. But, paradoxically, to get the ball up, you must learn to feel as though you are *hitting it slightly downwards*, as your swing travels forward to the target. To understand the statement "hit it down," look at parts A and B in Figure 6–1 and notice the angle of rebound (path) the ball takes as a result of the swing arc and loft of the clubface. (There are some additional technical reasons that control the angle of rebound, but

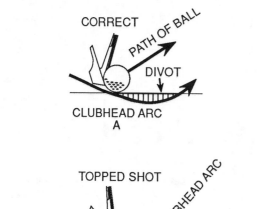

CORRECT

PATH OF BALL

DIVOT

CLUBHEAD ARC

A

TOPPED SHOT

CLUBHEAD ARC

PATH OF BALL

B

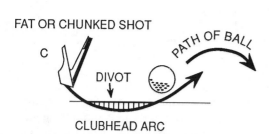

FAT OR CHUNKED SHOT

C

PATH OF BALL

DIVOT

CLUBHEAD ARC

Figure 6–1
Clubhead arc and resulting path of ball.

they do not contribute to one's understanding of the swing principle.) In 6–1A the proper arc is shown to reach its lowest point *after* the ball has been contacted. This is what we mean by "hitting down." Actually, we always should try to swing the club forward, "through" the ball to the target. But as you develop the correct weight transfer, the angle of the club shaft will be positioned slightly ahead of the ball when it's struck, to allow the club to continue downward before reaching the bottom of its arc. In this way it becomes both a forward swing and a downswing that takes a small grass divot.

You can see the approximate angle of rebound the ball will take because you forced the ball in your downward arc to work itself upward and onto the face. Once the ball is on the clubface, it has no choice but to go upwards. In essence then, your job is not to attempt to lift the ball, but to deliver the face down to and through the ball. As you practice your swing, it is advisable to check to see that your club is taking a divot, ruffling the grass, or (if on a mat) brushing the mat slightly in *front* or to the left of where the ball is resting.

Figure 6-1B and C show the arc that the clubhead takes when you try to *lift* the ball into the air. The result is that the bottom of the arc of the swing is reached *before* the club actually gets to the ball. In Figure 6-1B the leading edge of the club, rather than the clubface, strikes the ball. It makes contact above the ball's center and sends it rebounding in a downward direction. This causes "topping the ball," the most common error of the beginning player. Another shot that is in error for almost the same reason is shown in illustration C. Here the bottom of the arc again is reached before the ball is struck, but this time earlier in the swing (usually owing to an inadequate weight transfer). The result is the displacement of a great deal of turf behind the ball (called "chunking" or "hitting the shot fat") and an accompanying loss of force that sends the ball a shorter distance than it should travel—sometimes only a few feet.

Adjustments Among the Clubs

Now that you are aware of one of the fundamental concepts of hitting successful iron shots—swinging the club so that it results in a slightly downward and forward blow—let's look into the minor changes that are made when you switch from one iron to another. The principles of the swing remain the same for all full golf shots, but you must make some small but important adjustments.

The first adjustment is in the width of your stance. Longer shots require a bigger swing and therefore a wider base from which to secure balance. The positioning of your feet can also have an effect on the degree to which you can pivot your body. A stance that is too wide will restrict the turn both on the backswing and follow-through. Try it! Exaggerate the width of your foot placement and you will feel the restriction. The alignment of your feet also affects the turn. To see how this works, place your feet in an exaggerated closed position (the left foot ahead of your line of flight), and then see how far you can turn to the right. Reverse the line of your feet to an open stance (the left foot withdrawn from your line of flight), and try the same turn. It's obvious that your turn is much more restricted when you are in the open stance. A restricted turn will restrict the length of the backswing. On short-iron shots this is good; on long shots it is not.

The shorter-iron clubs are often used with what is called a *three-quarter swing*, which simply means that the club is swung approximately three-quarter as far back as a full swing with a wood. A full 9 iron shot would be a good example of a three-quarter swing. It is also a shot that may employ a slightly open stance to help restrict the pivot. Some top-level players play this shot from an open stance, others from square; but all use a shorter, more controlled swing than with a driver. Conversely, you need the greatest turn and therefore the longest swing and widest stance of the iron clubs when using a 1 or 2 iron. For all practical purposes, then, we can generalize that your swing is longer and your stance is slightly wider and more square on the long irons than on the short irons.

Another factor that the placement of your feet affects is the degree to which you can strike a downward blow to the ball. In a 9 iron, for example, the center line of the body ends up more to the left at address, encouraging the same at impact. Because the stance is not wide it is also easier to shift your weight to the left. Couple this weight transfer with a more upright swing as a result of having a shorter club, and you end up hitting the ball in a sharply descending blow. The 2 iron swing is less oblique because the club is longer and also because the wider stance does not permit a heavy concentration of weight on the left foot either at address or during the swing. A 2 iron shot therefore, will take less of a divot than a more lofted club.

Three Key Words for Iron Play

When you practice hitting balls, start with a 7 iron because it is about the easiest club to hit. A 5 iron would be second on my list of choices if a 7 were not available. Like all golfers, at the beginning you will produce your share of shots that will go skimming or bounding along the ground because they have been "topped." You can eliminate this mistake by concentrating on three key words, which can be applied to all iron shots. The three key words are *forward, downward,* and *through.*

When you say "forward," you should picture shifting your weight to the left foot and unwinding your trunk—using the back muscles, and pulling the club with your left arm. The word "downward" should simply keep you alert to the fact that you must deliver the face of the club down to the ball with your arms at extension. In this kind of swing, you should feel almost as if you are trying to "squeeze" or "pinch" the ball between the clubface and the grass. And "through" should be a part of every swing. Not "to" but "through." The result will be an on-balance full finish. It is important when considering these three key words that you first think "forward" and then "downward" and "through" together. Reversing this order and thinking "downward" first would cause you to chunk, or hit behind the ball.

THE WOODS

For many people the most satisfying feeling in golf is to catch a drive fully in the clubface and send it soaring far down the center of the fairway. Even the earliest written accounts of the game show that golfers were fascinated with distance. There was much made of prodigious driving feats, and long hitters were envied.

Though wood clubs are the long artillery in your set, they are also a source of frustration for many golfers. I have had people come to me for a lesson and say, "I can use the irons without trouble, but I just can't use the woods correctly. Should you swing differently with the woods than you do with the irons?" The answer, basically, is no. You employ the same principle for swinging in all full shots. Of course, you must make a few adjustments because of the length of the club or, in some cases, because the ball is teed; otherwise the mechanics are the same.

The Tee Shot

One solid fundamental to which you have just been introduced in the full swing is that players must hit slightly down and through on all iron shots. This may also apply to the fairway woods, depending on how the ball lies, but *not* to the tee shot where the ball is elevated in the air on a tee off the ground.

Overcoming distance is an important goal in driving a golf ball from a tee. Certainly you must keep the ball out of trouble, but a nice straight drive 150 yards down the fairway on a 400-yard hole is not nearly as advantageous as is a 250-yard drive on the edge of a rough. To get the most distance from your drives, tee the ball so that at least one-half of it is showing above the clubface at address. (Figure 6–2) You will want to position the ball far enough forward so that the ball is struck at the bottom of the arc of your swing. Hitting the ball at the lowest point of the arc, a level blow, decreases the backspin, which is a factor in controlling roll on the fairways. Just where you place the ball will depend on how strongly you shift your weight to the left, and where you feel you will get the best results. Generally, this is in line with your left heel or slightly back from it, about under the left arm pit.

In addition to positioning the ball differently on the drive, you should make two other small adjustments in preparing for the tee shot. First, stand farther away from the ball because the club is longer. (Use the same technique for body positioning that was described in Chapter 4.) Second, widen your stance so that the insides of your feet are about shoulder width apart. Since the tee shot employs the longest swing, it requires the most balance and therefore the widest stance. *But a note of caution:* Do not reach for the ball past your natural arm hang or stand with your feet wider than shoulder width apart. These are common mistakes for a new player.

Figure 6–2
Proper height to tee the ball.

Fairway Woods

The wood shot from the grass, called a *fairway wood*, is one of the most feared golf strokes of the novice player. There is no club in the bag with which he will top the ball more often. Many players put their fairway woods (3, 4, and 5) back in the bag and choose a 3 or 4 iron instead. This may be effective temporarily, but it is not smart for the long term. You should learn how to hit fairway wood shots, because you will eventually find them easier to use than long irons. A fairway wood, like a long iron, is hit only slightly down and through, more like it is being "swept" from the grass. The adjustments needed would be to stand farther from the ball than you would with a shorter iron, and to play the ball a bit farther back in your stance than you would with your driver—about two to four inches inside the left heel.

There is reason to believe that problems other than the added mechanical difficulty due to the length of the club might also make the fairway wood shot difficult at first. Psychologically, the player looks at the club, recognizes it as a wood, and instinctively swings it in the characteristic way he swings for his teed drives: Trying to sweep the ball up, he swings a little too high; trying for distance, he swings a little too hard. Because the ball is not teed, the fairway shot does not allow the player as much margin of error. Add to that the fact of mishitting the ball, which has been reinforced by past performance, and the player will usually tighten up just before making contact with the ball, thus shortening his muscles and pulling his club upward, away from and above the center of the ball. The result is a topped shot. To develop the confidence that is needed to hit the fairway wood shot well, choke the club to about the length of a 7 iron and imagine you are swinging the 7 iron for a few shots. Practice this until you have the confidence that the ball will get up into the air with the wood club if you just delivery the clubface a bit more *down* to it before following through. Then go to the full length of your club, let your arms hang relaxed, and make the swing.

Distance: The Wood Shot's Great Temptation

Distance is a prime objective of the drive, but how are you to achieve it? A friend of mine once described golf as "a game in which you try to hit a ball just a little harder than you are humanly capable of doing." That's what makes the woods difficult for many people. They try to hit rather than swing, and they try to hit too hard! The harder you try to hit the ball, the less chance you have of contacting it squarely. Frequent mishits produce an overall average distance that is actually shorter than one with a more controlled, repeated, steady swing. Since the wood club's extra length makes it more difficult to contact the ball squarely, try to make a full motion that gives you that "slinging" feel rather than a muscularly tight attempt to "hit hard." The term "slinging" implies winding, unwinding, and throwing or

Figure 6–3

A true swinging motion will bring you to a balanced, comfortable finish position. Fix this picture in your mind indelibly, and attempt to recreate it in your own swing.

releasing something. This concept may help you reduce arm and hand tension, and will produce a purer swinging motion.

Distance is the result of two primary factors (if we disregard, for the moment, the weight of the clubhead): (1) the velocity of the clubhead and (2) the squareness of contact. You may have heard someone exclaim after a particularly long drive that he didn't even try to swing hard. This can be explained quite simply. With a more free-flowing, yet controlled, swinging motion, you have a much better chance of making square contact with the ball and getting your best clubhead speed. Tension-filled efforts to hit home runs off the tee produce golf's most frequent "mistake shots," like hitting the ball on the toe or the heel, topping or skying it, or prematurely releasing the power from your wrists so that you either hit behind it or get "powder-puff" drives or big slices. Distance is best developed through the practicing of a well-timed, gradually accelerating, swinging-slinging motion. (Figure 6–3)

WHEN YOU GET OUT ON THE COURSE REMEMBER THAT:

A ball that goes in the air when you strike it is a result of the loft in the club-face rather than any attempt by you to lift it.

An open stance tends to restrict the length of the backswing, which is one reason it is used frequently in short-iron play.

The three key words to keep in mind when you start hitting iron shots from the grass are *forward, downward,* and *through*.

You should position your fairway wood more like your long iron than like your driver.

Full, uninhibited *swings* that you can repeat ultimately produce more consistent overall distance than muscularly tight attempts to "hit the ball."

7

THE SHORT GAME

where score can be influenced most quickly

In learning the basic short shots—the putt, the chip, and the pitch—you need to:
1. Develop some feeling for when each shot should be used.
2. Identify any gross change in execution from the full swing.
3. Be aware of the subtle changes in stance and address for each shot.

One of golf's more appealing characteristics is that it has managed to blend the demand for both power and finesse almost equally into a single game. No knowledgeable golfer denies the advantage of being able to strike the ball a great distance. Neither does he ignore the numerical importance of the shorter shots in the game, which are executed on and around the green.

PUTTING

Someone once suggested that there are two separate games played on a golf course: golf and putting. Golf is played in the air; putting along the ground. Their only common feature is use of the same ball.

There are several principles related to the laws of physics that govern a full swing, which can be accomplished only when a player performs specific patterns of action. But in putting, there are really only two imperatives. The style that you adopt to apply the essentials can take a wide variety of forms. By observing some of the great professional players on television, your conclusion may well be, "There is certainly more than one way to roll the ball into the hole." Before revealing the two essential fundamentals, however, let's see how important putting is in determining your score.

The putter is one of the most important clubs in golf. Don't let anyone convince you otherwise. You are allowed to carry a maximum of fourteen clubs in your golf bag. If you consider the approximate number of strokes it would take with each club to shoot 18 holes in 100, your pattern would look something like this: woods (both driver and fairway), 24 strokes; all irons, 38 strokes; putter, 38 strokes. Thirteen of your clubs would absorb 62 shots, and more than one-third of the strokes would be taken with the remaining club: the putter! (Figure 7–1) The better player you become, the greater percentage of your score will be determined by putting. The fastest reduction in score can invariably be accomplished by improvement on and around the green. That's the real scoring zone.

Two Imperatives

When I was in my teens, I once tried practicing a new putting technique on a rug, using as a target one of the little glasses you can buy at the supermarket that contain cheese spread. They have an opening slightly larger than the circumference of a golf ball. I was putting from a distance of eight to ten feet and averaging two or three "bull's-eyes" out of five. My mother, not being a golfer, questioned the point of my diversion. I explained that I was practicing my putting and asked her if she wished to try. She accepted and promptly grasped the putter in a most unorthodox way, stood in an awkward-looking position, and produced a terrible stroke that sent the ball right into the glass. Mumbling something about "beginner's luck," I retrieved the ball and placed it two feet farther from the glass for another try. She repeated her technique with exactly the same result. "That doesn't seem so hard," she commented. I was stunned, for I had been working on some very

Figure 7–1
Average percentage distribution of strokes.

complicated adjustments in my technique. Yet here was my mother, who doesn't even play golf, who gripped the club "wrong," stood "wrong," and stroked the ball "wrong," but rolled it dead into the glass twice in succession. She must have done *something* right! Then it occurred to me: (1) she delivered the putter on the correct line, with the face square to the target, and (2) she hit the ball hard enough to get to the glass but not so hard as to go through it. That's really all you have to do in making a putting stroke! And that is precisely what many fine players attempt to do when putting.

Deane Beman, former U.S. Amateur champion, PGA tour player and commissioner, and one of the game's greatest putters, has said that all he really attempts in his stroke is to keep the blade going toward his target and to develop some feel for the distance. It's that simple; but it's not that easy.

You must develop some kind of technique that will allow you to accomplish those two necessities in putting. The following method is *both* simple to understand and easy to learn. You may find another technique more to your liking, but try the following first. The answer to the decision on which method is right for you lies in the bottom of the cup.

The Technique

Standing with your feet about eight inches apart in a square stance, sole your putter in front of your left toe and rest it against your left leg vertically. Now let your arms hang in front of you and gradually bend forward at the waist, flexing the knees until your fingertips can touch the tops of your kneecaps. At this point move your right palm onto the grip directly. Your hand should assume any position that is comfortable in the palm and fingers, as long as it is directed toward the target. Now take the last three fingers and the thumb of your left hand and place them on the grip, sliding your thumb under the hollow made by the crease in the palm of your right hand. This will leave your left index finger free. Simply lap it over the fingers of the right hand, and point it in the general direction of the ground in the position that is most comfortable. This is known as the *reverse overlapping grip*. (Figure 7-2) In this position your right elbow will almost rest against the front of your right hip, and your left elbow will assume whatever spot that is natural and comfortable.

Place more weight on the left foot than the right to focus your balance and to discourage the strong tendency to sway. The club should be soled as though the ball were being played either inside your left instep or directly in front of your toe, depending on how much of your weight is on the left foot. You will notice that your left eye looks down on the ball almost directly. Adjust yourself to a reasonably comfortable position. Now you are ready to putt.

Keeping the Blade Square

One little trick I have learned, that may help you keep the putter blade square, is to place the ball about two feet from the hole. (This is to be done on a level surface.) Rest the blade of the club against the ball and square to the center of the hole. Then, keeping the blade squared, and without a backstroke, push the blade toward the hole briskly. The ball will leave the clubface, which should follow through from six to eight inches. If the terrain is flat and you have kept the blade square, the ball *must* go directly toward the hole. It has no other choice. Repeat this routine several times until you get some feeling for how hard to push. Then, still standing two feet from the hole, swing the blade back away from the ball three to four inches and with a smooth rhythm deliver the putter face to the ball squarely. This movement is made without action from the wrists. The wrists are in a fixed position so that the club, hands, wrists, and arms move as one unit. To continue the feeling of keeping the blade square, move the ball on the same line gradually farther from the hole. As you do so, increase the length of your backstroke slightly with each increase in distance. Concentrate solely on keeping the putter blade moving toward your target. On very long putts, it may be necessary to hinge the wrists slightly for additional power. As this complicates the task of delivering the clubface squarely, it should be done only when necessary. Don't assume that "wrist putting" is an unacceptable method, for it has been used

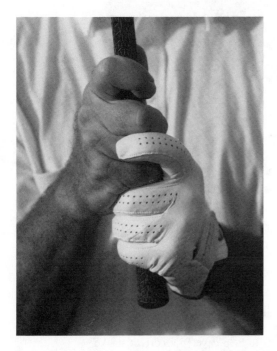

Figure 7-2
Reverse overlapping grip for putting.

by some of golf's finest putters. It is simply more difficult for a beginning player who should be learning to make the stroke in the least complicated style possible.

Some people unknowingly swing across the target line, close or open the face of the putter on contact with the ball, or both, sending it off the desired line. If you have this problem, practice the following exercise: Place a 2″ × 4″ on the green so that the inside edge lines up with the outside edge of the cup. Rest the heel of your putter on the board and let it swing back and forth like the pendulum of a clock. Put a practice ball on this path make a stroke and watch it drop into the cup. (Figure 7-3) Repeating this drill will give you the feeling of the blade moving toward the target.

Learning how hard to hit the ball is more difficult than simply learning a consistent path or keeping the blade squared. No one can teach you the secret to "how hard" to hit; it requires a certain innate touch or judgment of distance that some people find easy and others do not. Also, it requires a great deal of practice to judge distance on long putts over varying terrain and with fluctuating turf conditions. How do you know how hard to hit a putt? As a veteran professional once said, "Practice putt a few thousand times, and you'll 'know.' " Although this answer is fundamentally true,

Figure 7-3
Using a guide like this "Self-Teaching Board™" can help develop a correct stroke.

it is a bit unreasonable for the less experienced. Here are a few hints to help you for the time being.

It should be obvious that on short putts you take a shorter backstroke than on longer ones. But the correct length must come from a sense of feel. One method that I employ on long putts is to break the putt into halves. If I have a putt of thirty feet, I first take a practice stroke, trying to feel what effort I will have to give the putt to hit it fifteen feet along the same line; then I repeat this action but increase my backswing to get the proper pace for the full distance. That is the feeling that I try to develop just before preparing to strike the ball. These practice strokes should be made with a definite smooth rhythm. Whatever system you develop, it's a good idea to rehearse the feel before you hit the ball. When it feels right, putt.

Reading the Greens

Few golf greens are flat, even though many appear to be that way on television because of the elevated cameras. In fact it is more difficult to find a level green than it is to find an uneven one. Undulating greens, however, do not change the necessary mechanical fundamentals of putting; a square face, the right path, and the correct distance judgment. A sloped surface simply alters your aim. You still keep the blade square to the target, but the target is an imaginary one now, rather than an actual one like the cup. To allow for curve caused by the green's slope and gravity, you must *estimate* the line that the putt should take. Establishing this guessed line is called "taking borrow for the putt" or "reading the break." On long putts you should allow more borrow than on short ones over the same line, because gravity has a greater amount of time to work on the ball. (Figure 7-4) You will also find that you may tend to stroke the ball too easily at first when traveling

Figure 7-4
Judging the amount of "break" on the green takes practice and experience.

uphill and too hard when going down a steep grade. Practice these situations until you have a fairly good idea on how much break and effort to allow. Practicing your putting can be an enjoyable pastime either at the course or at home. Taking pride in your putting will certainly help reduce your scores—but performing those "few thousand" practice putts will help more.

CHIP SHOTS AND PITCH SHOTS

When you find your ball too near the green to take a full swing with any club, yet not in a position where you can putt, you must employ one of the short shots in golf, either the *chip* or a *pitch*. Their execution is different from that of the full swing because the stroke is abbreviated, sometimes no longer than that of a putt. The chip and pitch also employ slightly different techniques in the "setting up" to hit the shot.

The Chip

The chip shot is really just an elongated putt with a bit of loft at the beginning. You chip rather than putt when the grass on your line to the hole is too thick and will slow the shot or throw it off target markedly. Use a club with just enough loft to get the ball comfortably over the longer grass so that it can run uninterrupted to the hole. I recommend that my students limit their choices to a 6, 8, or pitching wedge for such shots. Far too many novices overuse the high-lofted club in situations where the running shot (which is easier to perform) is all that is necessary.

A great deal of the success of the chip shot depends on how you set yourself up. The shot is an iron shot, so you should hit it slightly on the downswing. Since power and long distance are not requirements of the chip shot, there is no need for a long backswing or any significant transfer of weight. In fact, the less complicated you make the shot, the better. With the ball placed between your feet (which are in an open stance position), put 75 to 85 percent of your weight on your left foot and leave it there. Just as with the full swing, you will find that with your weight to the left and hands kept ahead of the clubhead, the ball will be struck a slightly downward blow, which causes contact on the clubface and sends it up in the air.

Grip down on the club and let your arms hang so that they are almost brushing against your thighs. At address, keep your hands well ahead (to the left) of the ball and clubhead. (Figure 7–5A) The stroke on chip shots is very similar to that made in the putt. No wrist action is necessary unless the distance becomes a major factor. The only fundamental difference from the putt is that on the chip, the ball is struck a slight descending blow. This is facilitated by your placing your weight to the left, having the ball played farther back in your stance near the center, with your hands ahead of the clubhead throughout the shot. Setting your hands behind the ball at address or allowing your wrists to break on the forward swing in an effort to *scoop*

A

B

Figure 7–5

Stance and address for the chip and pitch
shots. A) Correct address: Player encourages
stroke down and through. B) Incorrect address:
player attempts to lift or scoop the ball.

the ball upward so that the clubhead passes the hands, is the most common error in the chip shot. (Figure 7–5B)

The Pitch

When the shot becomes longer and the ball has to be lofted into the air more, it is usually referred to as a *pitch shot*. The technique of setting up is almost exactly the same as for the chip: open stance, weight left, and hands ahead of the clubhead. In this shot as well, the ball is struck in a slight downward blow. Since the pitch shot usually requires more of a swinging effort to achieve the required distance, you must use a little bit of your foot-work action and a cocking of the wrists in execution. Even if some weight transfer is needed, keep at least 50 percent of the weight to the left throughout the swing. The best rule to remember regarding both the chip and pitch shots is to keep them simple by using only as much wrist action and weight transfer as is necessary for the distance played.

Knowing which club to use in a given situation is sometimes puzzling for the beginning player. A general rule of thumb is to use as little loft as possible and to allow the ball to roll when you can. (Figure 7–6) Some pros however, have developed such confidence in a certain club from continual practice (such as the pitching wedge or sand wedge) that they will use it for almost every shot around the greens. Perhaps if they had spent an equal amount of time practicing with the lower-lofted clubs, they might now be better short-game players. However, this is a moot point. For you, it is wiser to learn to pitch and chip with the clubs I've suggested, using the sand wedge for the most lofted pitching situations. Let your selection of the club be determined by each individual situation.

The Sand Shot

Most golfers have at best only a foggy notion of how to consistently execute a bunker or sand trap shot successfully. Hitting from sand is really not as difficult as the weekend player might make it seem. But you must know the mechanics and then spend a little time practicing them. Without the knowledge or practice, a sand trap experience can be very frustrating and stroke consuming. It certainly doesn't have to be.

A sand wedge makes sand play much easier. This is a club with a heavy, specially-contoured sole that deflects itself off the sand instead of digging into it too deeply. A pitching wedge or 9 iron could be used in a sand trap if you opened the face, but it would certainly be more difficult to use than the sand wedge.

The techniques for executing the shot are simple:

1. Establish a firm footing by working your feet into the sand.

2. Assume an open stance and position the ball near your left instep, farther forward than for a pitch shot.

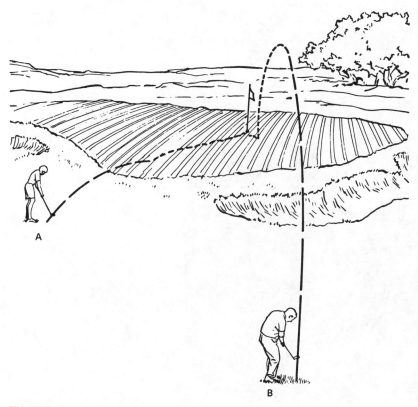

Figure 7–6
Club selection around the green. A) Chip or Chip-and-run shot: 6, 8,
or pitching wedge. B) Pitch shot: pitching wedge or sand wedge.

3. Place your weight to the left side slightly as you would for a pitch shot.
4. Pick a spot three to four inches behind the ball as your target.
5. Open your clubface so the leading edge will not "dig in" but rather allow the club to bounce.
6. Take a swing that moves the clubhead up in the backswing more abruptly and delivers a bit more downward blow than the pitch shot.
7. Complete the swing. (Figure 7–7)

The technique just described, the *splash shot*, is used when the ball is lying on top of the sand. The shot will stop quickly when it hits the green because it will have a great deal of backspin. If the ball is buried however, a different technique is used to "explode" the ball out. Square the face, move the ball back slightly, and move your hands ahead to lower the leading edge so it will dig. The deeper the ball is buried, the more dig you will need. Expect the ball to roll considerably after it comes out. In most cases, *swing through the sand. Do not chop your club into the sand and stop when you meet resistance* unless the ball is deeply buried and you must dig into the

Figure 7-7

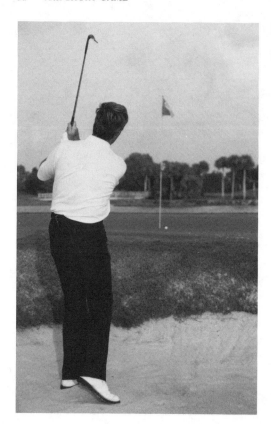

Figure 7-8
Sand trap shot—hitting your target.

3"–4"

A   B

sand with greater force. A few practice sessions in the sand will tell you how hard you need to swing.

The first step to success in hitting the greenside bunker shot is to understand that you *don't* hit the ball—you hit the *sand*, which acts as a buffer between the ball and the clubface. The trick to hitting the "splash shot" is to imagine that you are just trying to swing the club to a good finish over your left shoulder and to throw some sand on the green by swinging through a spot three to four inches behind the ball. (Figure 7–8 A,B) Focus your attention on "spanking" your club a little down and through this target during the swing. It will make the trap shot much simpler.

YOU SHOULD NOW REALIZE THAT:

From a scoring standpoint, one of the most important clubs in your bag is the putter. It should consume a significant amount of your practice time.

There are many things you *could* think of when putting, but there are only three mechanics that you *must* do after "reading" the green: Keep the putter moving toward the target with the blade square, and judge and hit the ball with the right amount of effort.

A chip shot is executed much like a putt except that the player's set up is changed. The pitch shot is an elongated chip using a more lofted club, often with wrists in a cocked position.

The club you select depends on both the situation and your ability to handle a club with confidence.

The trick to hitting a sand shot lies in being able to set up correctly, hit a spot in the sand the correct distance behind the ball, and to swing your club through to a good finish.

8

RULES AND ETIQUETTE_____

golf's laws and manners

This chapter will introduce you to:
1. *The historical development of the rules.*
2. *The principles on which these rules are based.*
3. *A practical application of both rules and etiquette.*
4. *The most commonly confronted rule situations.*
5. *Safety practices both on the course and during instruction.*

"It has been estimated that the golfer's chances of making a hole-in-one are much greater than the probability that he will read the rule book" (Graffis). This is unfortunate, for contained in the USGA's annual paperback *Rules of Golf* (available at all golf shops) is the wisdom and experience of generations of players who have attempted to make the game equitable for all, at every course in the world, under all possible conditions. One would think that the official rule book must compare to the unabridged *Webster's Collegiate Dictionary* in size! The fact is that it is small enough to fit comfortably in your back pocket or golf bag, right where it should be when you play.

DEVELOPMENT OF THE RULES

The first code of rules was born out of necessity in 1774. The gentlemen golfers of Edinburgh wished to have an interclub match with other players from surrounding golf establishments. Since each club had developed its own peculiar set of customs and traditions that were familiar only to its "own," some common understandings were needed to ensure an orderly match. Thus, a code of thirteen rules was established and sent to the contestants. Today, over two hundred years later, nine of those original rules are still in effect.

This early gathering of rule makers probably never considered the possibility that the rules for their local competition would be applicable to golfers all over the world. Contributed to and revised by The Royal and Ancient Golf Club of St. Andrews, the Edinburgh rules set the tone for the first universally-applied code in 1882. By 1902, the thousands of players who were active in the game had discovered numerous situations that were not covered in the rule book specifically. These cases were placed before a rules committee for decision. Similar committees aside from the R&A and the U.S.G.A., have been rendering decisions ever since.

NATURE OF THE RULES

There are five principles on which rules are based:

1. You must play the ball as it lies.
2. You must play the course as you find it.
3. You cannot advance the ball without striking it.
4. There is a basic difference between *match play* and *stroke play*. Match play is one player against an other player, hole by hole; no one else is affected. Stroke play implements total score; each player against the field. Consequently, rules differ for the two forms somewhat.
5. A hazard is special ground.

The basic purpose of the rules is simply to make sure that everyone plays the same game. Don't assume that golf rules always legislate against you. Just like laws, they exist not only to censure you, but also to protect and guarantee *your* rights. Let's take an example of a common rule that is violated frequently and little understood:

> Rule 13-4: Before making a stroke at a ball which lies in or touches a hazard. . .the player shall not: a. Test the condition of the hazard or any similar hazard. b. Touch the ground in the hazard or water in the water hazard with a club or otherwise, or c. Touch or move a *loose impediment* lying in or touching the hazard.

The purpose of a hazard is to penalize an errant, poorly played shot. If your opponent drives a wild shot into a bunker so that his or her ball is buried in the sand, he or she should pay the penalty of playing it from that spot. However, without the rule barring the touching of sand or soling the club, he could press the sand down or even dig around in the hazard without touching or moving the ball but improving his lie significantly. Similarly, in a grassed hazard, the player, before his shot, could use the club as a scythe. In either case, the spirit of the law has been violated. That's why hazards are sometimes called ''holy'' or ''untouchable ground.'' But there are some exceptions. (Figure 8–1)

GOOD MANNERS ON THE COURSE

Golf's unwritten rules are called *golf etiquette*. That is not to say that the rules of etiquette haven't been written down, but rather that they aren't really

Figure 8–1

In the middle of the picture you can see a ball resting in a footprint.
The rules do not allow relief from this condition or from the loose impediments on the right: a rock, stick, pine cone, and leaf, but you can
move the obstructions such as the rake, pencil, cup, and golf ball
sleeve on the left. If your ball moves in the process, replace it.

rules at all. They are suggestions. No one has ever been dealt penalty strokes
for poor manners on the course. You can't legislate good behavior—but you
can expect it!

Etiquette simply means consideration of the course and of others.
The problem is that when you are playing a new game, you may not be aware
of the particular behavior pattern that constitutes a breach of etiquette. I
wouldn't expect a brand-new golfer to know to stand so that his shadow
doesn't fall across the line of my putt, or where to stand when we are teeing
off, or when to repair ball marks and divots. But again, I'd expect him to
find out—soon! In fact, an experienced player has an obligation to teach
the novice this part of the game.

Golf is social, yet individual. You play with others and at the same
time compete against yourself and the course. For that reason you very seldom
mind golfing with a player of lesser ability. But you can't enjoy a round with
an ill-mannered player, regardless of his or her golf prowess.

LEARNING THE RULES

A golf rule book contains several elements, among them are:

1. Directions on how to use the book
2. The etiquette of the game

3. Definitions of key terms applying to the rules

4. A thorough cross-indexing

5. Changes in the rules from the year before

6. Special notes on such items as amateur status, gambling, lightning protection, and approved equipment

7. The rules themselves.

The rule book is small but not easy reading—that is, unless you are a lawyer. There are three rule books with illustrations that I recommend: *The New Rules of Golf*, by Tom Watson with Frank Hannigan published by the USGA, *Golf Rules in Pictures* by the National Golf Foundation, and *The Summary of Golf Rules* by the PGA. If you become a serious tournament competitor, you should definitely learn the complete rules. A new player needs to become acquainted with only the most common rules and etiquette situations. Listed below are (1) definitions of rules terminology, (2) examples of the more frequently violated rules and etiquette procedures, and (3) additional information pertaining to rules and conduct on the course in general. Given a golf rules and etiquette quiz, your full knowledge of this brief list would make you the slight favorite to outscore 75 percent of the nation's golfers. Applying this knowledge to your game will make golf more enjoyable for you, your companions, and your fellow golfers.

Common Rules: Definitions

Advice.   "Advice" is any counsel or suggestion that could influence a player in determining his or her play, the choice of a club, or the method of making a *stroke*. Information on the rules or on matters of public information, such as the position of hazards or the flagstick on the putting green, is not advice.

Casual water.   "Casual water" is any temporary accumulation of water on the *course* that is visible before or after the player takes his *stance* and is not in a *water hazard*. Snow and ice are either casual water or *loose impediments*, at the option of the player. Dew is not casual water.

Ground under repair.   "Ground under repair" is any portion of the *course* so marked by order of the committee or so declared by its authorized representative. It includes material piled for removal and a hole made by a greenskeeper, even if not so marked. Stakes and lines defining ground under repair are in such ground.

Hazards.   A "hazard" is any *bunker* or *water hazard*. (Figure 8–2)

Loose impediments.   "Loose impediments" are natural objects such as stones, leaves, twigs, branches, and the like; dung; and worms and insects and casts or heaps made by them, provided they are not fixed or grow-

A   B

Figure 8–2

Two hazards: A bunker (sand) and a water hazard.

ing, are not solidly embedded, and do not adhere to the ball. Sand and loose soil are loose impediments on the *putting green*, but not elsewhere. Snow and ice are either *casual water* or loose impediments, at the option of the player. Dew is not a loose impediment.

   Lost ball.   A ball is "lost" if: (1) it is not found or identified as lost by the player within five minutes after the player's side or caddies have begun to search for it; or (2) the player has put another ball into play under the rules, even though he may not have searched for the original ball; or (3) the player has played any stroke with a provisional ball from the place where the original ball is likely to be or from a point nearer the hole than that place, whereupon the provisional ball becomes the *ball in play*. Time spent in playing a *wrong ball* is not counted in the five-minute period allowed for search.

   Obstructions.   An "obstruction" is anything artificial, including the artificial surfaces and sides of roads and paths, except: (1) objects defined as *out-of-bounds*, such as walls, fences, stakes, and railings; (2) any part of an immovable artificial object that is out-of-bounds; and (3) any construction declared by the committee to be an integral part of the course.

Outside agency.   An "outside agency" is any agency not part of the match or, in stroke play, not part of a competitor's side, and includes a referee, a marker, an observer, and a forecaddie. Neither wind nor water is an outside agency.

Penalty stroke.   A "penalty stroke" is one added to the score of a player or *side* under certain rules. In a threesome or foursome, penalty strokes do not affect the order of play.

Provisional ball.   A "provisional ball" is played under Rule 27-2 for a ball that may be *lost* outside a *water hazard* or may be *out-of-bounds*. It ceases to be a provisional ball when the rule provides either that the player continue play with it as the *ball in play* or that it be abandoned.

Rub of the green.   A "rub of the green" occurs when a ball in motion is accidentally deflected or stopped by any *outside agency*.

Stroke.   A "stroke" is the forward movement of the club made with the intention of fairly striking at and moving the ball.

Teeing ground.   The "teeing ground" is the starting place for the hole to be played. It is a rectangular area two clublengths in depth, the front and the sides of which are defined by the outside limits of two tee markers. A ball is outside the teeing ground when all of it lies outside the teeing ground.

Through the green.   "Through the green" is all of the golf course with the exception of the teeing ground, the putting green of the hole being played, and any hazard on the course.

RULES FREQUENTLY VIOLATED

If you violate rules you are subject to penalty. The general penalty for match play (hole by hole) is loss of the hole; in stroke play it is a two-stroke penalty. The following violations all have the general penalty unless otherwise noted.

You Are Not Allowed to. . .

Take practice shots on the course.   Practice shots are not permitted during the play of a hole. Thus, a second drive from the first tee (commonly called a mulligan), is in violation of the rules (Rule 7-2).

Improve your lie anywhere on the course.   You may not improve your lie by touching the ball or by altering the condition of the course. This includes stepping down on the turf behind the ball in either the fairway or the rough, parting the long grass in the rough to get a better swing at the ball, and nudging your ball with the clubhead onto better turf. The most frequent and allowable exception to this rule is when, for the protection of the course or because of extremely poor playing conditions, the local course recommends the playing of *preferred* or improved lies, called *winter rules* (Rule 13 and Appendix I).

Change balls during the play of a hole. Unless your ball becomes damaged and unfit for play or is lost, you may not switch balls until the hole is completed. The use of a special ball for putting is a rule violation (Rule 5-3).

Play a ball from outside the course boundaries. If your ball comes to rest outside the stakes, fences, or walls that mark the boundaries of the course, you must abandon it and play another shot from the previous spot. The penalty for hitting out-of-bounds is a loss of distance plus one penalty stroke added to the two shots that were played (Rule 27). (Figure 8-3)

Concede putts to yourself of any length. The playing of a hole concludes when your ball drops into the cup, not before. You may not "give" yourself putts of any length. Only when an opponent in match play con-

Figure 8-3
You may not play a ball that is out-of-bounds.

cedes a putt are you permitted not to hole out (Rules 3-2 and 16). Penalty, disqualification.

Agree to waive the rules of golf.   You may not by mutual agreement with your partner or opponent agree to waive the rules or penalties associated with the rules in determining your score. Agreeing not to count a complete miss when intending to hit the ball would be an example of such a violation (Rule 1-3). Penalty, disqualification.

Sole your club in a hazard.   Since soling your club in a grass or sand hazard could improve the condition of your lie, it is forbidden by the rules and penalized by two strokes in stroke play, or the loss of the hole in match play (Rule 13-4). (Figure 8-4)

Receive from or give advice to your opponent.   Asking your opponent or another competitor during the play of a round what club he hit or how he played a given shot violates the rules. You are allowed to receive advice only from your partner and your caddie, and may give advice to your partner only (Rule 8).

Figure 8-4
The ball is resting inside the stakes and therefore in the hazard. You may not sole the clubface.

According to the Rules You May. . .

Remove loose impediments that interfere with your play.   As long as you don't move the ball in the process, loose impediments may be lifted. The exception to this rule is when both your ball and the impediment lie in a hazard (Rule 23).

Cause the ball to fall from the tee while addressing it, without penalty.   Penalties for moving the ball accidentally apply only when the ball is in play. A ball is not in play until a player has made a stroke on the teeing ground. Addressing the ball does not constitute a stroke (Rule 18).

Play a provisional ball when you believe yours to be lost or out-of-bounds.   When you are unsure as to whether your ball may have gone out-of-bounds or be lost, play a provisional ball. If you find that the original ball is lost or out-of-bounds, you may then play the provisional ball without having to walk back to the tee (you are lying 3). If you find your first ball and it is in play, you should abandon the provisional ball and incur no penalty (Rule 27–2).

Use any club you wish to play a shot.   No rule dictates the choice of clubs you must make. An iron or fairway wood may be used from the tee instead of a driver, or a putter may be used in a sand trap in place of a sand wedge.

Declare a ball unplayable and lift it under penalty of one stroke.   If your ball comes to rest in a place where it is unlikely to be hit successfully, you may declare it unplayable. Add one penalty stroke and take one of the following three options: (1) Drop the ball two club lengths away from where it rested but no nearer the hole; (2) drop the ball back away from where the ball lay originally, staying in a direct line with the pin, and going as far back as you need to get relief; (3) go back to the spot where the shot was played originally and play from that point. The player should choose the option that is to his/her greatest advantage (Rule 27–2).

Get relief from an "obstruction" with no penalty.   Obstructions are not on the course to add to the natural and artificial hazards of play. You may move an obstruction that interferes with your stroke. In the event it is immovable, find your nearest point of relief (no nearer the hole) and, within one club length of that spot, drop the ball (Rule 24). (Figure 8–5)

Lift and clean the ball on the putting green.   A player may lift and clean his ball on the putting green at any time. When lifted, the ball should be marked with a small coin at the backside base of the ball. The coin may be moved one or two putter head lengths over if it interferes with the line of a fellow player's putt, then later returned (Rule 16–1).

Figure 8-5
If the bench is moveable move the bench, otherwise move the ball.

ETIQUETTE FREQUENTLY VIOLATED

You Should Not. . .

Disturb another player who is in the process of making a stroke. Talking, moving around, and standing in a player's line of vision while he or she is making a stroke are all considered to be poor manners in golf.

Play a stroke until the players in front of you are clearly out of your reach. If your ball does appear to be in danger of striking someone, holler loudly and immediately the universal warning cry of golf, *"fore!"* If *you* hear someone shout *"fore!"* turn your back to the direction from which the voice came, cover your head, and make yourself as small as possible.

Damage the green with your equipment. Do not set your bag on the green, pull a hand cart across the green, or drag your spiked shoes, kneel, jump on the green, or step on the edge of the cup.

Hold up play on the course. It is good manners (as well as a rule) to play the game without delay. If you are not keeping up the normal pace of play on the course and there are players following you, let them go through to fill up the empty holes ahead. If your group loses a ball, wave the following players through while you search for it, letting them finish the hole before you continue.

You Should. . .

Leave the course as you found it; in good, or better condition.   Care of the course should be the concern of all golfers. You can do your part by replacing any divots you take on the tee or through the green, fixing ball marks on the green, and raking any sand traps from which you play. The more conscientious player will also go the ''second mile'' and repair damage done by other golfers. (Figure 8–6)

Observe the proper order of hitting.   When on the tee, recognize the order of hitting determined from the previous hole's low scores. During the play of the hole, let the player farthest from the flagstick play first. In your eagerness to play your ball, do not get so far ahead of the other players that you appear unconcerned over their results. On the other hand, be ready to hit when it is your turn.

Become familiar with etiquette for the putting green.   The putting green has its own etiquette situations. You should be aware that the following are violations of golf etiquette: standing so that your shadow crosses someone's putting line; leaving your ball in the cup after holing out; not marking your ball when it interferes with another player's stroke; failing to tend the flag for fellow players farther from the hole; stepping in someone else's putting line; and failing to repair your ball mark.

Figure 8–6
It ony takes a few seconds to repair your footprints with a rake to put the bunker back into good condition.

ADDITIONAL RULES INFORMATION

Carry no more than fourteen clubs.

Strike at the ball with the head of the club. Do not push, scrape, or spoon it.

Don't use artificial devices for measuring distance or weather conditions.

If your ball comes to rest on the wrong putting green, drop off (no penalty).

You may strike the flagstick from off the green without penalty. Striking it from on the green penalizes the player two strokes in medal play and loss of the hole in match play.

If you strike someone else's ball while playing on the putting green, you are penalized two strokes in medal play or loss of the hole in match play.

GOLF'S MAJOR PROBLEM: SLOW PLAY

A sign on the first tee of a well-known Scottish golf course reads, "A Round of Golf Takes 3 Hours." That's for eighteen holes, not nine. You will find that hard to believe and harder yet to accomplish on your first few rounds of the course. But it can be done when you know how to do it. Why, then, you may ask, does it sometimes take five or more hours to tour the local links?

One of the prime reasons is television. Too many amateur players mimic the professional ritualism that they see on their television sets on weekends. If you were putting for a quarter of a million dollars as a player might do on the final hole of the "Skins Game," you too might take a little extra time to survey the shot. But you aren't. Even if you were, it might do you more harm than good anyway. Alex Smith, two-time U.S. Open champion, had a favorite saying about putting: "If you are going to miss 'em, miss 'em quick!"

Putting is one obvious time-consuming activity on the course; there are other situations that are also "time wasters." You can overcome them if you apply these suggestions:

1. Know when it is your turn and be ready to hit. You may have to move slightly out in front of someone else who is playing his or her shot. This is an acceptable practice, provided you are to the side safely and are not disturbing the player.

2. When you hit the shot, see its finish and spot it with some landmark.

3. If walking, walk briskly between shots. The exercise will do you good.

4. When on the green, place your clubs or golf car between the green and the next tee so that you may leave directly. Leave the green immediately when finished. This is not the place to mark your scorecard.

5. Take your practice swings when you don't hold up your group or distract anyone.

It's true that golf courses are being built that are increasingly longer in yardage than they were at the time the three-hour round was the custom.

But the number of holes hasn't increased. It's still eighteen, and 500 extra yards of walking shouldn't take two hours. Interestingly, the world record for playing eighteen holes on foot on a course of over 6,000 yards in length was set in 1931 by Lee Richardson of Cape Town, South Africa. Richardson, a member of the South African Olympic track team, hit all shots with a single club, allowing the ball to stop before striking it again. He completed the round in thirty-one minutes, twenty-two seconds.

A LESSON ON SAFETY

If you think of golf as a fundamentally safe game, you are correct. Considering the number of players and hours spent on a golf course, the accident rate is low. The accidents that do occur, however, can be serious. Your awareness of the following safety hints could save you or some other player from an unnecessary and unfortunate accident.

During Play or Practice

1. Do not hit a ball when there is a chance that you might strike someone playing in front of or adjacent to you.

2. If you strike a ball inadvertently toward another player, shout *"fore,"* loudly and early enough for him to react. It's golf's universal warning cry of "look out" or "beware be*fore.*"

3. If you hear *"fore"* while you are playing, do *not* turn to see who yelled, but rather turn your back to the origin of the cry, cover your head, and make yourself as small as possible. (Figure 8–7)

4. Never approach a golfer from the rear who is addressing the ball or is about to make a practice swing.

5. Before making a practice swing yourself, on the tee ground or the practice range, look around you to see that no one is nearby.

Figure 8–7

Turn your back to the direction from which you hear the cry "fore."

6. Do not swing a club toward anyone who is standing near. Your hands often perspire, making the grip slippery and increasing the possibility that you might lose the club. In addition, clubheads have been known to crack and come off later in a practice swing.

In Unusual Weather

1. If an electrical storm occurs while you are on the golf course, get inside immediately. Several people are killed by lightning on golf courses each year because they did not take adequate precautionary measures. If you cannot get in, stay away from your clubs, which are natural lightning rods, and don't select a small, exposed shelter or a lone tree for cover. The safest places for shelter outside of a building are dense woods, at the foot of a hill or depression, or flat on the ground.

2. Be cautious in extreme heat about overplaying. The challenge of the game may tempt you to play in conditions that can overtax you physically.

During Class Instruction

1. If you are taking instruction as part of a golf school or class, carefully obey those safety rules that are explained to you in your early sessions.

2. Do not leave the range or hitting area to retrieve a ball or divot until the whole group has been released to do so.

3. Stop swinging when the instructor requests the group to do so. The temptation to hit "just one more shot" can lead to an injury.

When Riding in a Golf Car

1. If you find it necessary to use a golf car, keep your feet inside. Crushed ankles and broken legs are the most common golf car injuries.

2. Don't speed! Golf cars are easily tipped over, especially if someone is driving too fast and attempts to round a corner.

3. Try to avoid parking on steep inclines or crossing them laterallly.

4. Make sure that you know how to stop and start the car and how to operate and set the brakes before you get onto the course.

THIS CHAPTER HAS INFORMED YOU THAT:

It does not take long to learn the basic rules that govern the great majority of your playing situations.

The basic purpose of the rules is simply to see that everyone plays the same game.

A major problem that faces the game of golf is slow play.

Golf etiquette consists of a standard of good manners based on courteous and considerate treatment of others.

Though generally a safe game, golf participation has produced some serious accidents that could have been avoided with the proper precautions.

9

GETTING OUT TO PLAY_____

testing what you have learned

To help you over the on-course obstacles, this chapter will:
1. Suggest some pointers to prepare you for play.
2. Sketch an imaginary three holes played by a new golfer.

The preliminaries are over. In the first eight chapters you were introduced to the game of golf and given some essential information that should be of value to you in making golf fun, right from the start. Now it's time to play.

If you have been on the golf course a few times already, then you know that golf provides a great variety of situations to challenge you and enough satisfying moments to bring you back. Most of the shots demand a simple, normal execution of the swing on which you have been working, but some are special and have special results. For example, golfers dream of making a hole-in-one, and over 35,000 will achieve that dream this season. In fact, one player recently accomplished that feat his first time on a golf course—on his very first swing! Your concern on early trips around the course is less likely to be with holes-in-one than with questions such as: Will I hit the ball? Do I know enough about the rules? Will I be faced with shots that I have never practiced? Could I possibly make a par? Will I enjoy it? Will I be nervous? These questions can be answered only when you get out and play the game.

Call the course in advance to see if reservations are required. If they are, make your starting time by phone unless the course takes them in person only. In some cases, primarily at public courses in heavily populated areas, a deposit is necessary. If you are playing with someone but do not have a complete foursome, you may expect to be asked to pair up with two other players or to add a single to your group. This would be particularly true again of a public facility during peak playing time. If you absolutely do not wish to include strangers in your game (although you will find it turns out to be a pleasant experience 90 percent of the time), you might check with the course to see when it is least busy. If you are alone and have no one to play with, ask the shop or starter if they will pair you up with someone, telling them at what level you play so they can try to find a golfer close to your playing ability.

You may be unsure as to what equipment you will need and what is available at the course. If you don't own clubs, check to see if the course will rent equipment to you. Borrowing someone else's gear can be embarrassing and expensive if you happen to break or lose a club. Golf shoes, though an important part of your equipment are not required. Some courses, however, do have regulations on footwear. To be on the safe side, don't wear boots or any kind of spike-heeled shoes, cleated shoes other than golf shoes (for example, baseball or football shoes), or ripple soles that have sharply defined lines that might imprint the greens.

Balls, tees, and other accessories are in plentiful supply at almost every pro shop. Tell the professional or shop attendant what your skill level is and ask him, or her to suggest a type of ball for you to buy. You will need more than one!

After you have checked in at the pro shop and reported to the starter, you will know your turn on the first tee. If you have arrived at the course early enough, hit a few practice shots, providing facilities are available. If there is no range or practice area, spend your time putting and hitting some short chip shots. When the group before you is on the tee, you can go through your practice swing warm-up routine, but make sure that you are safely away from others. By doing this warm-up early, you will find that when it is your turn to hit you haven't occupied your entire time with introductions, finding a tee, getting your glove on, and locating a pencil for the scorecard. Now, let's play an imaginary three holes in which some of the situations that you may face on the course are confronted.

FIRST TEE PREPARATIONS

Identify your golf ball by name and number and inform your playing companions so that two of you don't use the same type of ball. If two balls are identical, mark them, or change one so they don't become mixed during play. (Figures 9-1, 9-2) Decide who shall have the "honor" of hitting first. This is usually decided on the first hole in a formal match by the flip of a coin, or in informal play by having whoever is ready to hit first do so. If there are players just ahead of you, it is sometimes customary to let the shortest hitters in your group play first so that you needn't wait as long for the group ahead to be out of range.

When it is your turn, tee your ball between or just behind the markers. If it is a hole with trouble close to the fairway, you may wish to start by driving with your 3 wood rather than with the driver, because the

Figure 9-1
Identify the type of ball you are playing before starting.

3 wood is easier to control and also makes it easier to get the ball airborne. Take a practice swing to refresh your swing feel. (A couple of swings are adequate—more, a waste of time.) Take a stance so that you aim the ball toward the part of the fairway that is farthest from the primary trouble on the hole. Visualize your ball going there. Then tell yourself: "Make your very best swing." There will be a tremendous temptation to *hit* the ball *hard*. *Treat that first tee shot more like the feeling of another practice swing*—make your *best* swing, not your hardest.

Figure 9-2
All brands are numbered.

If you are trying to think of the "hundred" details you learned about swinging—forget them! Just use this key: "I see.—I feel.—I trust." Then go out and have a good time."

PLAYING 1—A DIALOGUE

Well, the first stroke wasn't so bad after all. You had a little slice (a shot that curves to the right; one that curves to the left is called a *hook*), but it stayed in the fairway because you played to the left. It's still a long way to the green. The scorecard says this hole is 410 yards, so you will need another wood shot. One fellow in the group topped his shot; so after he hits, you can move up to your shot and be ready to go. You remember that these fairway woods should be hit just a little down, like a long iron; so on your practice swing, take a bit of grass to the left of the ball. Practice swing—now real swing the same way—got it in the air, great! Because you didn't catch it quite flush, it won't make the green; but it was a good shot for the first fairway wood. Your friends are looking in the rough (long grass) for a ball, so you should go over and help. The rules say that after five minutes you should declare the ball lost and play another from wherever the ball was hit before it landed in the rough. By the time you join your friends, the ball is found and the players then spread so as not to violate a rule of etiquette by standing too close to and distracting the person who is swinging. The shot out of the rough comes up short of the green and rolls into a greenside hazard (sand trap or bunker). The other two players' balls are on the green, and it's your turn. You select a wedge for the remaining thirty yards. There is a sand trap between you and the pin—your shot must get up into the air. In your eagerness to try to lift the ball, you leave your weight back on the right foot and end up *chunking* the shot (hitting behind it), dumping it only eight to ten feet in front of where you are. On the next try, you overcompensate and lift up on the shot (still keeping your weight back instead of to the left) and hit a low screaming shot that flies over the trap and overshoots the green by a good ten yards. The ensuing chip is short of the green by about a yard, and you are tempted to go up and chip again quickly with your wedge just to get on. Instead, you remember that a less-lofted club would be much better here keeping the blade close to the putting surface. Therefore, you switch to your 6 iron while your friend plays from the trap. You notice that when he takes a practice swing he hits the sand—a two-stroke penalty—but apparently he doesn't know the difference. You try to execute your chip shot as though it were a putt because you are only twenty feet from the pin. It comes up just about one and one-half feet from the hole—you're glad you didn't use your wedge. You must mark your ball—but someone suggests that you just *putt out* first, which you do successfully. You finish with a seven! But you *could* have been putting for a par if you hadn't flubbed the first pitch shot.

THE SECOND HOLE

The second hole is a par 5, 515 yards long, and it looks like 515 miles. You will probably have to hit hard on this hole. No, wait—that's the wrong way to think. Just three average-length shots with a wood could get you home: 3 × 175 yards would be on the back of the green. That's a better way to think about it. Your partners who had a 5 and a 6 on the first hole retain the honor. You shoot third, and your other companion who also had a 7 is last because he followed you on the first hole. (He didn't count the penalty in the sand. You'll tell him about it when you finish.) You tee your ball up, but in addressing it with your wood you accidentally bump if off the tee. Is that a stroke? (Figure 9–3) One of your more experienced partners tells you it doesn't count because there was no attempt to hit it. He's correct. Your tee shot, this time with the driver, is heeled badly and goes about 120 yards—tried to hit that one too hard! Maybe you'll stay with the 3 wood for a couple of more holes.

The last person in your group hits a big slice and exclaims, "Oh no, O.B.!" After you realize that he means "out-of-bounds," you look up the fairway and notice the white stakes bordering the trees on the right side. Hearing his ball hit the trees, you start to walk ahead when he says, "Wait, I'll hit a provisional." You recall that a provisional ball is allowed when a player hits a ball that *may* be lost or out-of-bounds. If the ball is in fact out-of-bounds, he plays the provisional and lays 3—a severe penalty for inaccuracy. His next shot is again down the right side but stops just short of the stakes. Had that one gone out, he'd have had to hit another and lie 5. When you

Figure 9–3

Accidentally moving the ball on the tee area prior to swinging is not a stroke as the ball is not yet in play.

reach your ball, you find it is in a poor lie, and you wish you could improve its position as one of the other fellows in the group did on the last hole—but you know it's against the rules. You must play the ball as it lies. This time, however, you use a 3 iron because it seems easier to get it up in the air from that poor lie. You hit the ball thin (almost topped) and leave yourself still a long way from the green. There is a search going on for the ball in the woods. As you cross the fairway, you notice that the group behind you is coming onto the tee. Mentioning this fact to one of your group, you step out of the trees, whistle, and give them a wave ahead with your arm.

After about a one-minute look, your companion spots a ball back down the fairway a few yards and identifies its make and number as those of the ball that was thought to be out-of-bounds. It turns out to be safe after all. It must have hit the trees and bounced back in. He is ready to play; but since the group behind hasn't quite passed, you must wait. The correct etiquette is to let the group through once you have waved them on. When they reach the green, your friend hits his original ball and lies 2, having abandoned the provisional, which was to be played only if the first one was out-of-bounds. You walk ahead to your shot and decide to use the 3 wood. The green is a little over 200 yards ahead, and the group is still putting; but you will have to hit your best shot to get there, so you just take a nice comfortable swing. You really connect, and it's going right for the players! *"Fore!"* The players ahead duck as the ball lands just short of the green, climbs the front bank, and rolls between them, on and over the putting surface. You apologize to them profusely as they leave the green for the third tee. "I didn't know I could hit it that far," sounds a little hollow when you say it; but they accept your statement, probably realizing that you are a beginner.

Behind the green your ball has come to rest right at the base of a tree. There's no way you can hit it. One of your foursome tells you to declare it an *unplayable lie*. (Figure 9–4) So you mark a spot two club lengths from your ball by putting a tee in the ground (you use your driver to measure), going no nearer the hole; stand, holding the ball at arm's length; and drop the ball within that two-club-length area. Add one penalty stroke, and now you lie 4—still not too bad. You have to clear a large bank to get back on the green, and therefore select your pitching wedge. Your practice swing gives you an idea about how hard you should hit it; but when the actual shot is played, you become afraid and let up in effort, and the ball fails to clear the bank and comes rolling back down at your feet. The next shot is too hard but fortunately hits the flagstick and drops about six feet from the hole. It would have gone clear over the green except for luck. But wait, is there a penalty for that? Not so, says a companion who anticipates your question. He explains that when you strike the flagstick from off the green, there is no penalty, but striking it from on the green results in a two-stroke penalty.

You must mark your ball because it lies in the path of one of your partners' putts. To mark the ball, you take a small coin from your pocket and place it right at the base of the back of the ball. If the coin had been

Figure 9–4

You may declare a ball resting in an "impossible" place as an unplayable lie.

on his line directly, you could have measured to the right or left with the length of your putter blade and moved it farther from his line. After marking your ball, you take a position behind his line so that you can see which way your putt will break. He steps up to his ball, then backs off and asks you to stand somewhere else since you are standing right along his line within peripheral vision range. He putts. Although he doesn't make it, he continues putting since he is not stepping in anyone's line in taking his stance and will move the play along faster. You follow, and your ensuing putt stops one foot short of the hole. Your companions say, "Pick it up." This means they will give it to you—conceding that you will certainly make it on your next stroke. This is acceptable in a match play tournament or in an informal game but would not be allowed in formal stroke-play competition. It's good practice to hole them all out. Your score is 8 for that hole with a penalty stroke! Well, no one ever said it would be easy.

THE THIRD HOLE

You have now moved to the bottom of the batting order with that 8. The fellows that you let through must have been held up because they are just starting to putt on this 145–yard, par 3 hole. But they replace the flag and wave your group on while they stop putting. This practice sometimes saves time on a crowded course by allowing the players following to be walking to the hole after their shots rather than standing while the group on the green is putting. Two in your party hit their shots on the green, while the third is strong, going over the green and onto the next tee area. You catch your shot well with your 7 iron but leave your ball yards short. You thought you would use the same club that the other fellows did, without considering the fact that they normally hit the ball farther than you do. You will have to learn your own distances for your clubs. You took a big divot on your tee shot. Someone throws it back to you as he starts ahead. You lay the divot back down the way it came out and step on it, knowing that it can grow back.

Because the green has a level approach to it, you elect to use the 7 iron again rather than a high-lofted club, since it seems easier to run the ball when the pin is farther back on the green. It works. You hit a good pitch-and-run shot, which winds up four feet short of the cup. Meanwhile, your partner has found that his ball rolled under the bench on the next tee. It is explained that this is an obstruction that can be moved, so he moves it and hits the ball with no penalty. Had the obstacle been immovable, he could have dropped the ball one club length away from the nearest point of relief (no nearer the hole) also with no penalty. Someone suggests that you learn the difference between "loose impediments," which are natural things like leaves, rocks, and twigs, and obstructions that are artificial.

Everyone holed their putts, and you are the only one left. The putt breaks a little to the left. You practice the correct effort with a preliminary stroke, step to the ball, and hit it just like your practice swing. It's in! No—it rimmed the cup. Almost a par! "You know," you say to yourself, "I rather like this game." (Figure 9–5)

Figure 9–5
There's nothing like the joy of success, whether it be over an opponent, the course, or yourself.

BY NOW YOU SHOULD REALIZE THAT:

Advance reservations are sometimes necessary, to play at your local course at peak times.

You should plan to arrive at the course early enough to allow for a suitable warm-up. On the first tee, you should forget the multitude of details about the swing and just try to picture and "feel" your very best swing.

The temptation to hit harder on a long shot or long hole should be replaced by a desire to make a good swing in a normal tempo.

There are definite procedures regarding rules, etiquette, and the simple logistics of being in the right place at the right time that you should be aware of before venturing onto the course.

10

PRACTICE _____

the way to success

In this chapter you will find:
1. Motor learning principles.
2. Reasons for practicing.
3. Ways to practice.
4. A form of practice aimed strictly at conditioning you for the game.

The objective of the first portion of this book was to provide you with enough essential information for you to enjoy golf your first few times on the course. But as you leave the beginner classification, you will begin to realize that there is a great deal more to be learned about this game. Problems will crop up for which you have no answers. Exposure to playing will create questions that probably did not occur to you at the outset.

You must now go beyond the basic fundamentals. The balance of this volume contains information of interest to people who are already golfers or who have decided that they are going to become golfers and are going to invest some time, money, and effort in the game. The following is only a small portion of what could be learned by the enthusiast, but it represents the first step beyond being a beginner golfer.

There is no such thing as a "natural-born" golfer. One may have natural ability, but there isn't a fine player in the game of golf today who hasn't spent many hours on the practice tee. The professionals realize that one hour spent in practice can generally reward them with more valuable information about the golf swing than four hours of playing on the course. Practice is an essential ingredient in the formula for golf success. For this reason it deserves the special attention of the serious golf pupil and the more advanced player. After reading this chapter, you may better appreciate why the solitary figure you see out hitting balls on the range when everyone else is playing is often next year's club champion.

Practicing is not all that much of a grind if you approach it correctly. As a matter of fact, some people prefer to practice rather than to play. A professional friend of mine has a sixty-seven-year-old student who hits practice balls by the hour. My friend's comment was, "What is he practicing for? He never plays in any tournaments." But in this case the pro discovered that the gentleman in question simply enjoyed the experience.

It takes a rare individual however, to practice for its own sake. There should be something for which you practice. If it is not an upcoming match, tournament, or outing, then your goal could be a certain score on the course or the conquering of a pesky fault. Goal setting crystallizes your practice plans and provides you with a built-in incentive.

Motor Learning Principles

There are certain principles of motor learning with which you should be familiar if you wish to receive maximum returns from your practice efforts:

1. Your emotional state may have a profound effect on your ability to learn or perfect a skill. Try to create a calm environment and a relaxed attitude. Composure is the key to effective play.

2. Incorrectly practicing a skill will naturally cause retrogression rather than improvement. In other words, practice does not always "make perfect." Practice makes permanent! (Figure 10–1)

3. Learning may be negatively affected if practice is carried beyond the point of fatigue. If you are extremely tired, stop.

4. For golf it is probably best to work on accuracy and speed simultaneously, since both are so essential to the skill. Speed can be sacrificed during drills in some cases, however.

5. Mentally rehearsing movement may help accustom you to it.

6. In general, many short practice sessions bring better results than long, widely scattered ones.

WHY PRACTICE?

Show me a golfer who plays the game at par or better, and I will show you a person who has played hundreds of rounds of golf and hit thousands of practice shots. Good golf is not luck or an accident—it is, for one, a great deal of practice. When we speak of "good golf" in this sense, we mean very good golf, par golf. The "good enough just to enjoy it—to heck with the score" level of golf can be attained fairly quickly with some decent instruction and a little practice. (Figure 10–2) But most people have a desire to improve, no matter what level they have reached. It would be grossly unfair and inaccurate even to hint that it is a relatively simple matter to become a truly fine player. Your improvement in the game will be measured in close proportion to the amount of effort you put into it.

One of golf's most publicized practicers was a professional named Henry Picard. Picard often had the feeling that he could in one stroke ac-

Figure 10-1
Golf is a wonderful game for practicers.

tually hole out shots from 150 yards after an intense practice session. The results he gained through practice were an example to many other pros, and have impacted scoring today. Picard's greatest influence may have been exerted on one of his young friends, the immortal Ben Hogan. As a fledgling pro, Hogan had been told by several golf teachers that he didn't stand a chance on the tour with *his* golf swing. Picard's encouragement and Hogan's

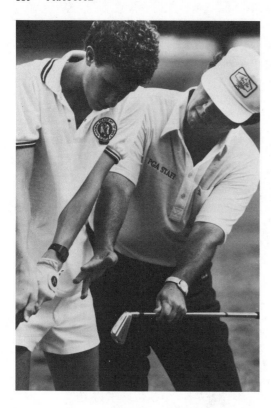

Figure 10–2
Starting golf when you are young is a distinct advantage: starting with good instruction makes it more so.

painstaking practice helped Ben make golf history. Since then, the likes of Gary Player, Arnold Palmer, Jack Nicklaus, Tom Watson, Tom Kite, Curtis Strange, and Nick Faldo have proven the value of dedicated practice.

PRACTICE CORRECTLY

If you practice anything long enough, you can become reasonably automatic in its repetition—bad golf swings included. What a sorry waste of effort it is to see a person practicing and playing with golf fundamentals that make major improvement literally impossible. A man who had been playing golf for a number of years came to me for a lesson. He was very discouraged, to the point of quitting the game, and was skeptical about his chances to improve. But his wife had bought him three private lessons. I have never seen anyone who took such an unorthodox grip on the club; the results could only spell disaster. After three shots I couldn't contain myself and said, "Look, why not just let your arms and hands hang naturally without twisting them into such contortions, and hold on firmly with the last three fingers of your left hand. Then swing the club." (Discounting the grip, the fellow actually had a reasonably good swing.) He tried the correction and produced a shot that, although not spectacular, seemed miraculous to him. "Why, I haven't hit one that good in thirteen years!'' he exclaimed. And he meant it. With some additional minor adjustments in his grip, he continued to hit good shots.

The point is, it would have been a complete waste of time for this man to trudge faithfully to the practice tee, dragging along those bad habits. In his case it took only a few minutes to learn something positive and correct on which to practice. After his other two lessons and occasional checkups, he developed a sense of the correct mechanics involved in the preparation and execution of the golf swing. Only then did he receive handsome rewards for the practice time he spent. You can do likewise if you find yourself a competent teacher, develop an understanding of the basic fundamentals, and decide what you need to practice. Then the time that you do spend practicing will be much more rewarding.

WHERE TO PRACTICE

There are actually several possibilities open to you for a practice site. The most obvious, of course, is the public driving range. If you have limited time and can afford it, a driving range can most certainly be a convenient practice facility. In addition to allowing you to rent balls, they usually provide free clubs, are sometimes covered to protect you from rain, and are occasionally heated in cold weather.

Or you can look for some nearby open space where you could hit practice balls without endangering anyone: a remote area of a park, an unused playing field, an area bordering the golf course, or any place that has short or no grass and few people. If you find such a spot, then buy some used balls from the golf course or use your old ones that have become unfit for play but are acceptable for practice. Purchase a shag bag (one used for holding practice balls) or obtain an old airline flight bag, bowling ball container, or overnight case in which to keep your practice ball supply. Owning your own practice balls can be a strong incentive to practice if you can find a place to use them.

Not all practice needs to be done outdoors or with real balls. One alternative to the driving range or open field is the indoor net. A great deal can be learned about the swing made indoors where the golfer is concerned not about the flight of the ball but rather the feel of the swing. Some fine players have developed at indoor winter golf schools where the motto was, ''The swing's the thing.''

HOW TO PRACTICE

Driving ranges should be renamed. The title encourages people to hit shots with their drivers exclusively, as if it were the only club in their bag. Most of these people are trying to see how far they can propel the ball. This really isn't practice—it's just an expensive form of exercise. Any relationship between that kind of practice and score improvement is purely coincidental. If we started calling these areas "practice ranges" or "learning centers" rather than driving ranges, we might be on the right track. Also, a good deal of your practice should be spent on the shots around the green. (Figure 10–3) I require my students to spend at least 50 percent of their practice time on the short game.

What you should try to develop in any practice session is a feeling that is comfortable and repeatable—one that you could repeat a thousand times if you had to. To acquire that feeling, first do a warm-up that consists of swinging two or even three clubs at a time. The added resistance provided by the extra club or clubs will slow your tempo and, because of the added weight, makes you more aware of the centrifugal force. After you complete this warm-up, start hitting shots with your short clubs and work up to the woods gradually. When you get to your driver, be just as concerned with accuracy and rhythm as you were with your irons. With all that open space in front of you, there is an almost uncontrollable urge to just "let it fly," drive after drive. If you succumb to this temptation, you will find yourself overswinging and losing the repeatable controlled feeling that you have been trying to build. Treat your tee shot swing much like the swings for the rest of your clubs. A former U.S. Open champion once remarked that he never tries to hit a long drive consciously. Nonetheless, he undeniably hits many.

As much as possible, make your practice sessions simulate the real game. Hit from the grass when possible; use a target on all your shots; alternate clubs, sometimes going from a wood to a short iron as you would in the playing of a hole; imagine that you are playing a particular shot on a

Figure 10–3
Practice on the short game can reduce scores faster than any other use of the game.

hole at your home course; then watch the results. Be competitive in practice, either practicing with someone else in contest fashion or setting up standards and tests for yourself.

If you apply these practice tips to the fine instruction that is available to you through books, professional teachers, and school instructors, better scores will soon be coming your way.

CONDITIONING YOUR BODY

It is fairly obvious that practicing by hitting the golf balls and swinging will help you improve. But there are other kinds of practice related to the game that may be of value. The question arises: Will you play better golf if you are stronger and in better physical condition? Will certain exercises improve your game? The honest answer is that no one really knows because this subject has not been researched thoroughly. But from my experience, I would emphatically say, "Yes!" The right exercises given to the right people for the right reasons can, I'm convinced, help one's golf.

Most right-handed golfers, for example, are weak in the left arm and hand. Some are so weak that they are prone to the following mistakes: loosening the club with the last three fingers of the left hand at the top of the backswing or near impact; excessively bending the left arm; failing to adequately use the left side. These fundamental errors in swing could probably be helped by simply strengthening the left side.

I conducted a laboratory study that supported the importance of strength in driving a golf ball for distance. Distance, although important to golf, is, of course, only one aspect of the game. However, since longer drives do correlate with lower scoring, it is logical to assume that strength plays some role in good golf.

Strength alone is not the only physical factor that influences the distance picture. In fact for some, flexibility and timing may be more important if they already have the strength. When you consider the many factors that affect this one aspect of golf—driving—and then add the other parts of the game, such as chipping and putting, attitude, and experience, you realize the difficulty with saying that such and such an exercise will make you play better golf. But certainly the stronger, more flexible player possesses greater potential to score.

Some of the exercise suggestions that are supposed to help your golf have ranged from simply making a fist to doing one-hand extension push-ups on the finger tips. In the former case, anyone could do it; in the latter, probably one person in 50,000 could. I seriously doubt if either of these suggestions for increasing strength would help your golf more than any of a hundred other types of exercises.

I am firmly convinced that a lack of general body conditioning can be a handicap to a person hoping to play good golf. (Figures 10–4, 10–5, 10–6) In my study on the drive for distance, the evidence clearly indicated

Figure 10–4
My own strength training includes work on a
Distance Builder.

Figure 10–5
Gym-in-a-Bag, also for strength.

Figure 10-6
Flexibility exercises are very important if you tend to be tight, and as
you get older.

that increasing age was accompanied by increasing physical deterioration and
decreasing ability to hit a long drive. To what extent physical deterioration
or lack of fitness affects the rest of the golf game is still a matter of conjecture.

It is reasonable also to assume that fatigue can have an effect on
playing golf, which requires such a high degree of precision. If this is the
case, then a person highly conditioned for endurance activities will be better
able to ward off the prospect of deteriorating play due to fatigue.

Without knowing your case specifically, it would be difficult to
prescribe the best type of exercise program for your golf game. In my book
Super-Power Golf (Contemporary, 1984), a complete training program for
increased distance is offered. Briefly, what appears to be a most sensible and
economical approach to the problem of conditioning your body for golf is
this:

1. Any program that improves your overall strength, flexibility, and endurance will probably help.

2. Using the principle of overload (or moving increased weight through the
same motions you make in a golf swing) seems sound. You might take an object heavier
than a normal golf club—such as a weighted club, bar from a barbell, rake, or home-
made weighted device—and swing it like your golf club.

3. If you use weights, concentrate on the legs, forearms, back, and hands,
while deemphasizing the biceps, upper shoulders, and chest. (Heavy development in
the latter areas restricts your swing.)

4. Be sure to include walking, jogging, running, or skipping rope—something that works your legs and builds endurance.

5. Do sit-ups for the abdominal muscles, lower-back exercises, and work
on a good stretching program. This will help protect you from the back problems
that plague even the tour players.

CONDITIONING YOUR MIND

The term "psychosomatic" is generally applied to illnesses that are induced or nurtured by a psychic cause. Those psychic forces that we think can actually work against us physically can also be turned around to work for us. Book titles like *The Power of Positive Thinking, You Can Work Your Own Miracles,* and *Powers of Mind* suggest the positive approach to a sort of psychosomatics in reverse of its usual context.

You should begin to condition your mind in a positive way before you even get to the golf course. Research studies have clearly demonstrated that a form of mental practice, that is, spending some quiet time thinking of a physical task, such as shooting a free throw, making a springboard dive, a downhill ski run, or performing a gymnastics stunt, can be as effective as and sometimes more effective than the same amount of time spent in actual physical practice. Of course there are some conditions to this, including the matter of clearly understanding the proper technique. It has been demonstrated conclusively that mental practice can be a useful aid in learning physical skills.

Mental practice in the form of positive visualization to improve your swing has been suggested in golf literature from as far back as fifty years ago. In a book I coauthored with Dr. Richard Coop called *The New Golf Mind* (Simon & Schuster 1978) we detail the broad extent to which the mind affects shot-making. This imaging in the mind can have a positive effect on your performance and is indeed worth your attention.

Some type of mental visualization is practiced by the touring professionals consistently *during* their play. For example, one player may try to visualize his swing for the next shot while he is walking toward it. While putting, players may try to see the ball actually proceed along the intended line and drop into the hole before they putt. Others try to do the same with their short shots around the green, mentally picturing the anticipated trajectory and noting where the ball will land and how it will roll, before they even step up to make the shot. Players will also picture the techniques of other particularly good performers. (Figure 10–7) This is practiced so widely that it is hard to discount the fact that it is effective. Unquestionably, it is an important part of the game.

But even of more importance than the images one conjures up to play a shot are the images one has of himself or herself as a competitor, as a putter, as one being able to handle pressure—anything that relates to a player's overall golf performance. *The greatest gift I could give an aspiring player would be to help him or her develop a strong self-concept.* A good self-image breeds confidence, and confidence promotes mental and physical relaxation. Since tension is the great destroyer of a golf swing, feeling good about one's ability to play the shot gives the best chance for success. Where does this "good feeling" come from? It comes from previous success in practice and play, focusing on that success, and pushing out the thoughts and images of any previous failures. Simply, it comes from dwelling on the positive rather than the negative.

Figure 10-7
Watching Tour players can be a great learning experience in creating
positive mental imagery.

You Should Have Learned that Your Golf Game Depends upon the Realization that:

There is no "easy way" to become a proficient golfer. Practice is one of the essential ingredients to make progress toward that goal.

Practice alone, without a knowledge of the proper mechanics, is an inefficient expenditure of time and energy.

Worthwhile alternatives to practicing at the driving range are using a net, swinging in the backyard, using available open space, and practicing mentally.

The practice sessions in which you are working on the full swing should be devoted to developing a consistently repeatable stroke.

Short game practice should occupy at least 50 percent of your practice time.

Physical conditioning and mental practice are two extra types of work routines that will help your game.

There *is* power in positive thinking.

11

CORRECTING GOLF'S MOST FREQUENT ERRORS

topping, chunking, slicing, and hooking

Because everyone hits bad shots, you now need to know:
1. What causes these shots.
2. How to make fundamental corrections.

One of the first things you learn when hitting a golf ball is that all the shots don't go where you want them to. In fact, more of them deviate from the intended line than stay on it. Improvement in the game comes through decreasing the percentage of shots that fall into this latter category. The four most common "bad" shots are the *topped shot*, the *chunked (fat) shot,* the *slice*, and the *hook*.

Even the greatest golfers hit these bad shots at times. But the difference between the fine player and the poor one is that the fine player doesn't hit them as often, and when he does, he knows how to correct them. The poor player will chronically repeat the error season after season, frequently for his whole golfing lifetime. This form of self-torture is quite unnecessary since there are cures for all known golf "diseases."

Even when you know the causes and cures for errors in golf, it is sometimes difficult to select the *right* correction. Obviously, the touring professionals whose livelihoods depend upon being able to make good golf swings know their swings in detail. But pros also have *their* experts to whom they go when in trouble. The reason is that we often can't feel or see in ourselves the mistakes that we are making. It frequently takes someone with a trained and objective eye to spot our problems. Be extremely careful, however, about taking advice from well-meaning "semi-pros." If you encourage it, and sometimes even if you don't, you may be deluged with tips on curing your current golf ailments. A friend or even a complete stranger may try to force on you a pet cure that worked for him. More than likely it is compensation for another error and may be totally unrelated to your basic problem. You will save yourself much money, time, and frustration if you politely reply that you are going to have a lesson the next day with a professional to have the problem taken care of. Then, *do it!*

TOPPING

If you have watched much golf, you know that in all cases, except putting, a successfully executed golf shot travels in the air initially. Those that bound along the ground are considered undesirable. It is probably this urge to get the ball "up" that causes people to try and scoop it or lift it into the air. In previous chapters you have learned that the clubface is built with loft that will elevate the ball if you just deliver the clubface on the ball. To help you to swing slightly down and through the shot, you should develop a footwork pattern that concludes the swing with a positive weight transfer to the left. (Figure 11–1) People who try to scoop the ball *up* generally finish the swing either flat-footed or with their weight back on their right sides. Four key words can help a person overcome this serious fault: *left, forward, down,* and *through*. Think of those four keys, in that order, before you swing. Say to yourself: "I must shift my weight to the *left* while allowing my left arm to lead so the shaft is angled *forward,* allow the clubhead to travel *down*, and continue *through* to a good finish." By programming your thoughts in this way and using the following tips, you should not have further problems topping the ball.

Check Points to Help Avoid Topping

1. Take a practice swing that takes a slight divot of grass in front or to the left of the ball. Try to do the same thing when you get to the shot. This demonstrates your correct transfer of weight to the left.

Figure 11–1
On a full swing always finish with your weight fully to the left and your right foot on the toe.

Figure 11-2
The left arm has collapsed because the right is tight in trying to lift the ball. The result is a topped shot.

2. The right hand is the culprit that tries to scoop the shot and results in pulling you up in the air, away from the ball. Be more conscious of using your left side to feel a slight downward pulling motion before continuing to the target. Actively using the left arm helps keep it in the desirable extended position. Failure to do so encourages it to collapse. (Figure 11-2)

3. Check to see that you are not reaching too far for the ball; rather, your arms should hang comfortably after you have bent from the hips. In this way you will use your body more actively, rather than just your arms and hands.

Other causes of topping—like trying to hit too hard, bending your left elbow, and picking your head up—are related to not getting the weight shift to the left foot and not using your left side properly so that it arrives in proper sequence, before the clubhead.

CHUNKING (HITTING THE SHOT FAT)

"Chunking" means hitting behind the ball, displacing a lot of earth but moving the ball only a short distance. It is a first cousin to topping in that the causes and cures are almost the same. If you frequently hit behind the ball, check the following:

Check Points to Help Avoid Chunking

1. Are you trying to hit the ball before you have transferred your weight to the left foot? An early release of power by prematurely uncocking the hands can cause the shocking experience of contacting the earth before the ball, much to the displeasure of your wrists. Unfortunately, this often discourages people from doing the very thing they should be doing: hitting slightly down through the shot. Again, you need to emphasize the lead of the left side and the transfer of weight. This will help you get your swing sequence in order.

2. You may have placed the ball too far forward in your stance so that the bottom of the arc of your swing is falling at the correct spot but the ball isn't there to be hit. Check your practice swing to see that the ball is played so that its front side corresponds to the point where your divot mark begins. This will be about four inches inside the left heel.

3. Check to see that you haven't gotten too close to the ball in your address. Your arms should be in an extended hanging position. The arms will tend to extend naturally during the correct swing. If they are bent at address, the club may not have room to clear the ground. But standing too far away is more of a problem than standing too close.

4. Lowering your head or swing center during the swing could also cause you to make your initial contact with the ground rather than with the ball, though it is a less common reason.

SLICING

Once a person has learned to get the ball into the air, the slice (a shot curving from left to right) is by far the biggest problem he will likely face. It is the nemesis of thousands of golfers, many of whom have come to believe that it can't be cured. This, of course, is ridiculous. Anyone can learn to hit the ball without producing a slice.

One of the main reasons for a mass-population golf disease like the slice is that the body and hand positions in the swing that encourage a slice are more comfortable and more instinctive than those that produce the straight shot or the hook. Man usually seeks the way of least resistance in everything he does; golf seems to be no exception. The slice was also, in a sense, inadvertently built into some older methods of teaching, which in some quarters still persist. By "built in" I mean that the accepted technique of rolling the face open and then trying to close it during the swing requires the player to have excellent timing plus strong and supple wrists before the slice disappears. Unfortunately, a great number of people are simply unable to correct their weakness. And so the slice remains a prevalent error plaguing the average golfer.

Check Points to Help Avoid Slicing

1. A slice is caused by hitting the ball with the face open to the line on which you are swinging. This can happen when, 1) the face is square to the target but the swing travels to the left, that is, outside to in, or 2) when the path is correct but

Figure 11-3

The shoulders are aiming left, which encourages the swing path to travel the dark arrow across your intended path. When the face is square to your intended line but open to your swing path it applies a "cutting action" or sidespin to the ball making it slice.

the face is open, looking to the right of the path (Figure 11-3). Any correction you make applying to a slice should work toward alleviating one or both these faults.

2. Check your swing line first. Put a club down along your line of flight and see if the swing "feels" like it is traveling from the inside of that line slightly out and then on toward the target. In actual fact, to hit the ball straight the club must approach the ball from inside the flight line and then go directly on the line toward the target before continuing around into the follow-through. It will feel as though the clubhead is coming from inside the line of flight and continuing out slightly to the right of the target before finishing the swing. If you find that you are crossing the line of flight before striking the ball (hitting from the outside in), then make the following corrections:

Get your swing back in sequence, which basically is (a) weight back to the left side, (b) arms swinging down and forward as hips turn to the target, and (c) hands releasing the power by allowing forearm rotation, upper body rotation, and uncocking of the wrists. When the hands start to release ahead of the weight shift and arm swing, the club is thrown outside the flight line, cutting across that intended path. When the face fails to match that path and stays open to it, a slice is produced. By getting the swing back in sequence with the body, forearms and hands releasing later in the downswing, you will approach the ball from inside the intended flight line rather than outside. One other element you have to look for is the alignment of your body in relation to your intended line. Most important is your shoulder line, as it has the strongest influence on swing path. If your shoulders point to the left, they encourage your swing to go that way. The hips and feet influence the shoulders and therefore should be considered. Basically, an open stance, or one with the left foot pulled back from the line of flight, encourages slicing by helping to produce an outside-to-in swing path. So get your body alignment correct and your sequences in order. Then the path will be correct.

3. If your swing is already coming from the inside or if you have just worked on this fundamental and are still slicing, then you have one more place to look—the clubface. In order to square it, take a closed face with your left hand (that means three knuckles on the back of your hand showing). Swing the clubhead away in a square position for the first ten to twelve inches, square rather than turning the toe

open (to the right). At the top of your swing, when your wrists are cocked, make certain that the back of your left hand and your wrist are flat or close to flat. If the left wrist however is cupped so that wrinkles appear under the wrist joint rather than beneath the thumb, the face of the club is probably open and the back of your left hand should be flattened close to the level of the forearm. When you enter the hitting area on the downswing, try to see that the back of your hand is facing the target rather than looking up at you. You may at first have to close the face with your hand forcibly by turning the toe of your club over in a counterclockwise rotation. Make certain that the clubhead is traveling toward the target. After a few attempts, it should become more natural rather than forced. Let your forearm rotate and release the clubhead to come over and through the shot. Feel the weight of the clubhead! If your wrists feel stiff, you haven't made a complete release. Should you start hooking the ball severely, adjust the left-hand grip back to two knuckles and make impact with a flat rather than a collapsing wrist.

These swing checks will work if you do them. I've had people working on their slice with these techniques who said, "It doesn't work." But when I watched them perform, I had to tell them, "It didn't work because you didn't do it." You may sometimes feel as though you are doing what you are supposed to; but if the ball does not react correctly, then you are not.

HOOKING

It has often been said that good golfers are more likely to hook rather than slice. The only thing good about a hook is that it may indicate a certain strength in the hands and wrists of the beginner, assets that are later quite helpful in becoming an accomplished player. An uncontrolled hook can get you into just as much trouble, if not more, as a slice. Its only advantage is that it will generally produce more distance than a slice because it has less backspin. The causes and cures for this shot are just about the reverse of those for the slice.

To hook a ball, you must either have the face closed to the intended path or hit it markedly from inside out with the face square. It is impossible to hook a ball in any other way. Unlike the slice, it is much harder to hit the ball from an exaggerated inside-out position, and so this fault is much less common.

Check Points to Help Avoid Hooking

1. Look first to your grip. If either hand is turned too far to the right (clockwise) on the grip, so that the "V's" are pointing outside your right shoulder, move it or them more on top of the shaft toward the chin. Most commonly, the right hand is placed too far under the shaft.

2. If your grip appears to be correct, then look at the top of your backswing to see if you have hooded (closed) the clubface. If the face of your club is pointing directly to the sky, it is closed. The result will most likely be a sharp hook. An arched (opposite to cupped) left wrist will cause the closing; therefore, flatten your left wrist instead of letting it fold toward the inside of your forearm.

A. Ball above your feet.

B. Ball below your feet.

C. Uphill lie.

D. Downhill lie.

When the ball is above your feet, the tendency is to pull or hook to the left.

To adjust, simply aim more to the right of the target. Also check to see that your club can clear the ground in a practice swing. Take one club stronger than usual for the distance and swing comfortably. Gravity will try to pull you backward, particularly on a hard swing.

When the ball is below your feet the tendency is to push the ball or slice.

To adjust, simply aim more to the left of your target. Make sure that you are standing close enough to the ball that you won't top it, and make a special effort to stay down with the shot. Let your weight be more to the heels and sitting, since gravity wants to pull you forward.

In an uphill lie, the tendency is to pull the ball and hit short of your target.

To adjust, use at least one club stronger than usual for the distance and possibly more if the grade is severe. Keep your weight to the left side and play the ball a little forward in your stance. Aim slightly to the right. Fight gravity by working up the hill to the left in the swing.

In the downhill lie, the tendency is to fade the shot to the right and to skull or top it.

To adjust, aim to the left and let the ball fade. Play the ball slightly back of center in your stance and stay down with the shot, following the contour of the ground. Level your shoulders more to the slope of the ground.

Figure 11-4

3. Finally, the most common source of the hooked shot is letting your right hand overpower your left during the swing. If the left arm quits or doesn't do its share, the force of the right hand will close the face of the club and hook the ball. To keep this from happening, take a firmer grip with the last three fingers of your left hand and maintain the grip you started with in your right. It is quite common to change or regrip in the right hand during the swing. You have much less chance of hooking if your right-hand grip is made in the fingers correctly rather than in the palm and fingers. Use your left arm in the swing aggressively so that the right doesn't catch up too soon and collapse the left, causing the swing path to go left.

UNEVEN LIES: A CAUSE FOR BAD SHOTS

One of the factors that can encourage a golfer to hit a shot that is topped, chunked, hooked, or sliced is finding his ball lying on uneven terrain—a common experience on most courses. By making adjustments in your stance and alignment, you can combat these tendencies to err. Study the following situations and become familiar with the correct adjustments (see Figure 11–4). For a more complete treatment of the problems we face in playing the game and how they can be handled, refer to *Sure Shot* by Gary Wiren with Dawson Taylor, published by Contemporary.

As You Correct Your Shots, You Should Remember That:

The techniques for curing the topped shot and fat shot are often the same.

Slicing is caused by hitting the ball with an open face, by cutting across the intended line of flight from outside in, or a combination of both.

If you are swinging correctly by approaching the ball from inside your intended line of flight and are still slicing, then work on closing the face by altering the position of your grip, to one that produces a more closed face, flattening your wrist at the top of your swing, or reducing grip tension to allow more aggressive hand action and forearm rotation.

The most common cause of the hook is a dominant right hand caused by an improper grip.

You should seek advice from a competent golf professional if you are unable to cure your golfing errors.

12

WHAT SCIENCE CAN TELL US ABOUT GOLF

sorting fact from fiction

This chapter aims to:
1. Relate the facts known about the game that are based on scientific evidence.
2. Apply these facts, in a final mechanical analysis, to that elusive skill known as the golf swing.

The body of knowledge that has been developed around the game of golf in the last 500 years is largely empirical—the result of personal observation and experience. Teaching methods and playing techniques have evolved as an art rather than a science. Golf has, for the most part, eluded the onrush of scientific investigation. But the "unscientific" approach to problem solving, even in golf, is largely a thing of the past. The modern golfer is intelligent enough to insist on knowing the "why" of the golf swing in addition to the "how." The research that has been completed in the area of golf has supported, to a large extent, the practices of current teaching professionals. In some cases however, traditional thinking has been challenged directly, and a need for some rethinking on several points has developed.

THE BRITISH GOLF STUDIES

By far the most complete scientific investigation of golf yet completed was the research work sponsored in the 1960s by the Golf Society of Great Britain. Spearheaded by a wealthy real estate investor, Sir Aynsley Bridgland, the society attracted some of the finest researchers in the British Isles. Their disciplines included medicine, anatomy, biomechanics, physiology, physical education, ergonomics, ballistics, physics, and engineering. Some of their findings are presented in *The Search for the Perfect Swing*, by Cochran and Stobbs (1968). More recently, in 1990, the First World Scientific Congress on Golf was held in Scotland at St. Andrews University. The following are some highlights from both the book and the congress.

Equipment

A drive that carries 200 yards in the air when the ball is at 71 degrees Fahrenheit will carry only 185 yards at 32 degrees. This supports the practice of changing balls at each hole in cold weather and substituting one that has been warmed in the player's back pocket from body heat. (Artificial warmers for golf balls are not legal in competition.)

The best combination of club weight to produce maximum distance is best determined by personal experience in hitting balls since everyone's return pattern and strength is different.

A longer-shafted driver (up to about four inches over the standard forty-three inches for men) would give one an advantage in distance without significant loss of accuracy if his or her timing is correct.

Putters weighted at both the toe and the heel have less chance of hitting errant putts when they strike the ball with an off-center blow.

The speed of the greens one plays may dictate the best weight of putter to choose.

Equipment can be manufactured specially to reduce a player's tendency to slice, hook, top, or whatever.

The Full Swing

The legs and trunk must play a greater part in producing distance for the top-class player than the arms and hands, since some thirty pounds of muscle is necessary to generate clubhead speed of around 100 miles per hour. (Figure 12–1)

The ball travels fifteen to twenty yards down the fairway before the player has a chance to react to what he felt at impact.

Althought the left-arm swing alone is truly representative of the mechanics of a model golf swing, it can produce only three-quarters of the distance of a properly timed two-handed hit.

The difference between a well-timed hit and a poorly timed hit is only about one-fiftieth of a second.

A one-degree error in the clubface aim at impact will result in an approximate 8-yard error by the time the ball travels 200 yards.

The clubhead moves its fastest at a point in the swing just before it catches up to the hands.

Approximately 80 percent of males and females align their shoulders and clubface to the right when aiming at a target of 200 yards.

Putting and Chipping

For right-handed players, the right hand seems to have greater sensitivity and is therefore important in developing touch for the short game.

Figure 12-1

Tour star Tom Watson has developed a business-like, no frills type of golf swing that utilizes the legs and trunk to good advantage and generates a swing speed of approximately 116 m.p.h.

The ball is on the putter face for a long putt about the same length of time as for a drive (roughly one-half a millisecond).

Deliberate efforts to add topspin or backspin to a putt are of little or no value.

Even a perfect putting machine is able to hole only 50 percent of its putts from a twenty-foot distance, owing to the irregularities of a typical putting surface.

APPLYING SCIENCE TO THE SWING

Science usually deals with details. Thinking of details during your swing, particularly as a new player, can be ruinous. Therefore, the earlier description of the golf swing in this book was based largely on feel rather than on detail. At this point it may be worthwhile to explain the details behind the feelings.

The golf swing takes approximately two seconds to complete. In that time it is virtually impossible to consider the physical details of what is or should be happening in sequential order. Those people who try to think their way through a swing fail miserably. It is important, however, to be knowledgeable concerning certain details of the swing and to understand it from a purely mechanical standpoint. Without this understanding you will find it difficult to make sound adjustments and corrections when your swing goes sour.

The objective of a full swing is to deliver the clubface in such a way that the ball travels on the intended line of flight and is carried the correct distance. There would be no real problem hitting a ball straight, if you needed to move it only a few yards. Evidence the short putt, which is rarely missed by more than a matter of inches. But in the full golf shot, the need for distance complicates the problem of accuracy. For example, in order to make the ball travel far enough to get to a par 4 green in two shots, you must generate considerable clubhead speed and deliver it to the ball squarely. A physical law that is essential to developing that speed is centrifugal force. Applied to the golf swing, it is the force that tends to impel the clubhead outward from the center of rotation. This outward "pulling" action helps the swing attain its maximum arc, thereby providing it with the greatest potential for speed. Given the same rotational force then, the wider the arc, and the greater the speed. This fact theoretically gives taller people with long arms an advantage in achieving distance. You could create a similar increase in mechanical advantage with longer clubs. It doesn't guarantee distance however, because a tall person or someone with an extra long club may not be able to generate much rotational force or to deliver an accurate blow. Nonetheless, this information concerning the importance of attaining a wide arc should cause people to consider both their equipment and their techniques.

It is to this feature, a wide arc, that one of the PGA Tour's long drivers, Davis Love, III, attributes his incredible distance. The value of having an extended left arm, through the hitting area in particular, then becomes more apparent. This longer lever simply has more potential for producing force. It should be maintained in a relatively extended position throughout the backswing because it is more conducive to consistency than bending the elbow markedly and then trying to return the arm to the ball extended again.

The length of the backswing can also affect potential velocity. A longer swing will involve more muscles and give the player more time to build up speed. Diminishing returns occur, however, when on the backswing the club drops more than 5 degrees below a level parallel with the ground. At this point additional force is needed to overcome gravity in bringing the club back up; and more importantly, the player generally loses the control that is necessary to make solid contact with the ball.

Another scientifically based principle in the swing is observed in the momentum that is developed in the clubhead on the downswing. When the left arm reaches a point approximately forty-five degrees from a vertical line running through the ball, the wrists and hands begin to make their contribution to the summation of forces that was initiated by the hips and followed by the shoulders and arms. Not until the left arm reaches a point less than ten degrees from vertical should the wrists allow their final bit of energy to be released. This is known as the *delayed hit*. It represents maximum power and efficiency in the golf stroke because it succeeds in blending the forces of trunk, arms, and hands into one flowing motion. The delayed hit builds its speed by one force contributing its effort just as the other force is begin-

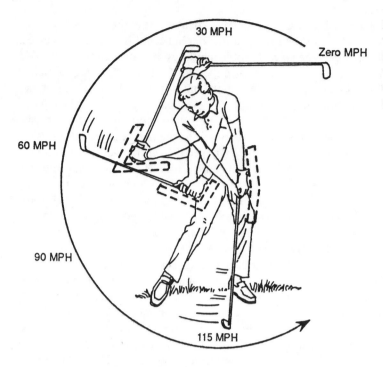

Figure 12–2

The delayed hit. Speeds indicated are arbitrary values approximating the speed of a strong player's swing.

ning to diminish (see Figure 12–2). This gradual building of force and speed in its most efficient progression is known as *timing*. Its presence can be observed in a well-executed football pass, baseball throw, or javelin hurl. The sequence of lever action is the same essentially—hip rotation, and arm and shoulder action, with the wrists and hands coming in last.

The follow-through is only an indication of what went on before. An abbreviated follow-through is a strong sign that clubhead speed was diminishing before the ball was ever struck. It suggests a hitting-*at* movement rather than a hitting-*through* action. An artificial continuation of the swing for form's sake after its energy has been spent is worthless. But if the natural pulling action developed by the club's velocity carries through to a strong, full finish, you have probably maintained your maximum clubhead speed in the hitting zone. In that case a good finish means something.

With such a forceful swing (traveling over 100 miles per hour), it is necessary to have a strong base of support. Too wide a stance affects the rotational range of your trunk and shoulders, while too narrow a stance does not give you adequate equilibrium for such a powerful effort. A stance of approximately hip width is conducive to the best mechanics for a full distance swing.

Owing to the importance of having to make a weight shift toward the target, you will need adequate footing. With friction alone, it is difficult to maintain the foot's stability against such a force. Golf spikes are needed. Without the added traction offered by cleated shoes, the feet may slip and cause a loss of both power and accuracy. If you have ever tried to throw a ball and had your back foot slip just as you were applying your drive off that foot, you may understand what is meant.

The mechanics of golf are difficult to perform consistently because you deal with a striking instrument much longer than those used in other sports and one that travels at much higher speeds. Once the club is delivered, it has a comparatively small hitting surface that must strike the ball squarely to achieve a satisfactory result. These factors alone make it clear why it takes considerable time to master consistency in hitting a golf ball. On the other hand, a golf ball sits still. It does not require the same hand-eye coordination or highly sensitive reaction time as does a sport like baseball or tennis. Also, the adjustment for height is built into the equipment. It requires the player to exercise only preliminary deliberative judgment, not a split-second adjustment. If it were not for these latter factors, golf would be too difficult to play. As it is, the game is stimulating, but not out of reach for most people. I hope that you rise to the challenge.

AFTER READING THIS CHAPTER, YOU SHOULD KNOW THAT:

Equipment design and material can have a definite effect upon the results you get when striking a golf ball.

The margin of error in golf between a good and a poor shot is very small.

Understanding the mechanical principles involved in making a golf swing should help you to make sound adjustments in your game.

A longer lever, either in the arm or in the length of club, has a potential for greater force in the swing.

The follow-through in golf is simply an indication of the quality of the swing that has preceded it.

The summation of the physical forces of the body in a well-timed sequence and employed in the golf swing is known as the *delayed hit*.

You can indeed become proficient at the game of golf.

THE LANGUAGE OF GOLF___

Ace: A hole completed in one stroke.

Address: The process that a player goes through in positioning himself and the club for a stroke.

Approach shot: A full stroke played to the putting green, usually made with a medium or short iron.

Apron: The bordering grass around the green, not as short as the green but usually shorter than the fairway. Sometimes called the "fringe."

Away: The ball deemed farthest from the hole, to be played first.

Best ball: A type of play in which the lower score of either of two partners is counted in the match.

Birdie: One stroke less than the par for the hole.

Bite: Backspin imparted to the ball, which makes it stop abruptly.

Bogey: One stroke more than the par for the hole.

Break of green: The slant or the slope of the green, sometimes called "borrow," when considering the amount of curve to allow for.

Bunker: A hazard in the fairway or rough or near the green, which may take the form of a mound or depression and can be filled with grass or sand. The term is often used synonymously with "sand trap."

Caddy: A person who carries a player's clubs and otherwise assists him in play in accordance with the rules.

Callaway system: A method of handicapping players who have no established handicaps by applying the score a player has just made to a predetermined formula; used particularly in one-day outings for infrequent golfers.

Carry: The distance that a ball travels in the air before striking the ground.

Casual water: A temporary accumulation of water that is not meant to be played as a hazard.

Chip shot: A short and usually low-trajectory shot played to the green.

Chunking (Fat shot):   A swing in which the clubhead strikes the ground before the ball and thereby decreases the distance of the shot.

Closed clubface: One in which the face of the club points to the left of the intended line of flight.

Closed stance: A position of the feet in which the right foot is withdrawn from an imaginary line across the toes that runs parallel to the line of flight.

Cocked: A position of the wrists in which the left wrist is flexed laterally (toward thumb side) and the right wrist is hinged dorsally (back of hand toward forearm).

Divot: A piece of sod taken from the ground by a player's stroke, which should be replaced and stamped down.

Dogleg: A bend in the fairway that crooks similarly to the hind leg of a dog.

Dormie: A player or side that is ahead in a match by as many holes as there are left to play; used only in match play competition.

Double bogey: Two over the par for the hole.

Double eagle: Three under the par for the hole or, most commonly, a score of 2 on a par 5 hole; also called an "albatross."

Down: The number of holes or strokes that a player is behind his opponent.

Draw: A shot that curves slightly from right to left; slight hook.

Driver: The number 1 wood club that is most often used from the teeing area.

Dub: A poor golfer or a poorly hit shot.

Duffer: A player with poor skills.

Eagle: Two strokes under the par for the hole.

Explosion shot: A forceful shot made in a sand trap, which displaces a large amount of sand and forces a buried ball upward and out of the trap.

Fade: A shot that curves in flight slightly from left to right.

Fairway: That portion of grass between the tee and green that is kept closely mowed so as to provide the ball a good lie.

Flag or flagstick: A marker placed on the green, indicating the location of the cup.

Flat swing: A technique of swinging that employs a less vertical and more horizontal swing than normal. The backswing may stay below shoulder level.

Flight: The path that the ball takes in the air; or a division of players in a tournament according to playing ability.

Follow-through: The remainder of the swing after the ball has been hit.

Fore!:   A warning cry to anyone who stands in danger of being hit by a ball.

Foursome: Four players playing together in a group. It technically means two players playing against two others, but with each side playing only one ball between them, hitting alternate shots.

Grain: The direction that the grass grows and lies on the putting green. It can have a marked effect on both the break and the distance allowed for in a putt.

Gross score: The actual number of strokes a player has taken before his handicap is deducted.

Halved: A hole that each player or side in match play competition has played in the same number of strokes. It means a tie, or one-half a hole for one side with one-half a hole for the other.

Handicap: A rating of a player's ability relative to shooting par; used to equalize competition between players of unequal ability.

Hazard: In general use, any natural obstacles on the course, such as trees, ponds, ditches, bunkers, etc., but more specifically, by rule, bunkers and water hazards.

Heeled shot: A shot hit near or off the portion of the club that attaches to the shaft.

Hole high: Ball that has come to rest even with the hole but off to one side.

Hole out: To complete the play of the hole by hitting the ball into the cup.

Honor: The right to drive or play first from the teeing ground; determined by the lowest score on the previous hole or on the first tee by the flip of a coin.

Hook: A golf shot that curves from right to left. A "duck hook" or "smothered hook" would be one that is particularly low to the ground and curves sharply to the left.

Lie: The position in which the ball has come to rest on the ground; or the angle that the shaft makes with the ground when the club is soled properly.

Links: Originally a seaside golf course, but now used frequently to mean any course.

Loft of the club: The amount or degree of pitch that is built into the clubface.

Loose impediments: Natural objects that are not fixed or growing, such as twigs, loose rocks, pine cones, or leaves.

Match play: A form of golf competition in which each hole is a separate contest. The winner is determined by holes won rather than total score.

Medalist: The player who has shot the lowest qualifying round for a tournament; also, the player with the lowest score in a team match.

Medal play or stroke play: A form of golf competition in which the winner is determined by the lowest score for the round. The rules of golf differ slightly between match and medal play.

Mixed foursome: A group of four players made up of two men and two women.

Mulligan: The common but illegal practice of driving an extra ball on the first hole in the event that the original ball is not to the player's liking.

Nassau: A method of scoring a match based upon the allowance of three points: one for the winner of each nine and one for the winner of the total eighteen holes.

Net score: A player's score after having subtracted his handicap from his gross, or actual, score.

Obstruction: Anything artificial or man-made, whether erected, placed, or left on the course, except objects defining the course boundaries, such as stakes, fences, or walls; also, artifically constructed roadways or pathways.

Open stance: A position of the feet in which the left foot is withdrawn from an imaginery line across the toes that runs parallel to the line of flight.

Open tournament: One in which both professionals and amateurs can compete together.

Out-of-bounds: Any area outside the boundaries of the course as defined by white stakes or some other designated marker.

Par: A theoretical score representing a standard of excellence based on the length of the hole, and allowing for two putts.

Penalty stroke: A stroke added to a player's score for an infraction of the rules or to gain relief within the rules.

Pitch shot: A short, lofted shot made with the intention of getting the ball onto the green.

Press: To attempt to hit the ball harder than usual; or to double a bet previously made for stakes by initiating a new and second game from the time of the press to the end of the nine holes being played.

Provisional ball: An extra ball that is hit when a player feels that his original ball may be lost or out-of-bounds.

Pulled shot: Shot that travels to the left of the intended line.

Pushed shot: Shot that travels to the right of the intended line.

Rough: The long grass and other vegetation that border the fairway and surrounds the green.

Rub-of-the-green: The occurrence of a ball that is in motion being stopped or deflected by an outside agency.

Sand wedge: A club with a heavy, wide sole that is designed principally to be used in sand bunkers.

Scotch foursome: Four players divided into two teams, each team playing one ball, each partner hitting alternate shots.

Scrambler: A player who shows exceptional skill around the green after demonstrating loose play in getting there.

Scratch player: A player who plays around par consistently and has a handicap of zero.

Shanking: Hitting the ball with the neck (hosel) of the club, making it travel in an oblique direction to the right.

Skying: Hitting the ball high in the air only a short distance, when it was intended to travel much farther.

Slice: A golf shot that curves from left to right.

Sole: The bottom of the clubhead; or the act of resting the bottom of the clubhead on the ground at address.

Square stance: A stance in which a line drawn from the toe of the right foot to the toe of the left foot runs parallel to the line of flight.

Stance: The position of the feet and body when a player addresses the ball.

Summer rules: The regular playing rules of golf that do not allow a player to improve the lie of his ball except under special conditions.

Tee: The wooden or plastic peg on which the ball is placed at the start of a hole; or the area from which a player starts the play of a hole, more correctly called the "teeing ground."

Tee markers: The markers placed on the teeing ground that designate the point from which play of the hole begins.

Through the green: All of the area on the course with the exception of the teeing ground, the green, and any hazard.

Toed shot: A shot that is struck on or near the toe of the club.

Topped shot: A rolling or low-bounding shot that is caused by striking the ball above its center of gravity.

Winter rules: A situation in which the course is not in top playable condition; therefore a player is allowed to improve the lie of his/her ball.

SELECTED REFERENCES AND READINGS

There are over 1,500 books that have been written on how to swing a golf club. Obviously you cannot read them all; even if you could, too many approaches lead to confusion. Below are some good instructional as well as some excellent noninstructional books that are noted with a *.

There are now a large number of golf instruction videos available as well which can be very useful to those trying to improve their game. For the most complete listing contact the Booklegger, P.O. Box 2626, Grass Valley, CA 95945

AULTMAN, DICK, and KEN BOWDEN. 1975. *The Methods of Golf's Masters*. New York: Coward, McCann & Geoghegan.

BALLESTEROS, SEVE, and JOHN ANDRISANI. 1988. *Natural Golf*. New York: Atheneum.

*BROWNING, ROBERT. 1955. *A History of Golf*. New York: E. P. Dutton.

*COCHRAN, ALASTAIR, and JOHN STOBBS. 1968. *The Search for the Perfect Swing*. Philadelphia: J. B. Lippincott Co.

DANTE, JOE, and LEN ELLIOTT. 1962. *The Four Magic Moves to Winning Golf*. New York: McGraw-Hill Book Co.

*DOBEREINER, PETER. 1973. *The Glorious World of Golf*. New York: McGraw-Hill Book Co.

GEIBERGER, AL, with LARRY DENNIS. 1980. *Tempo*. Norwalk, Conn.: Golf Digest.

*GRIMSLEY, WILL. 1966. *Golf—Its History, People, and Events*. Englewood Cliffs, N.J.: Prentice Hall.

HOGAN, BEN. 1957. *Five Lessons—The Modern Fundamentals of Golf*. New York: A. S. Barnes & Co.

HOGAN, CHUCK.   1986. *Five Days to Golfing Excellence* Lake Oswego, Oregon: Merl Miller & Associates Ltd.

HOWE, WINSTON, and WILL LAMPLEY,   1988. *Swing Dynamics,* Denver, Colo.: Howe & Lampley.

JACOBS, JOHN, with KEN BOWDEN.   1972. *Practical Golf.* New York: Quadrangle Books.

JONES, ROBERT TYRE (BOBBY).   1966. *Bobby Jones on Golf.* Garden City, N.Y.: Doubleday & Co.

KOSTIS, PETER.   1982. *Inside Path to Better Golf.* New York: Golf Digest.

LEADBETTER, DAVID.   1990. *The Golf Swing.* Lexington, Mass.: Stephen Green Press.

LOPEZ, NANCY, and DON WADE.   1989. *Nancy Lopez's Complete Golfer.* Chicago: Contemporary Books.

MURPHY, MICHAEL.   1972. *Golf in the Kingdom.* New York: Dell.

*NATIONAL GOLF FOUNDATION.   1986. *The Easy Way to Learn Golf Rules.* Jupiter, Fla.: National Golf Foundation.

NICKLAUS, JACK, with KEN BOWDEN.   1974. *Golf My Way.* New York: Simon & Schuster.

PALMER, ARNOLD.   1965. *My Game and Yours.* New York: Simon & Schuster.

PALMER, ARNOLD, and PETER DOBEREINER. 1986. *Arnold Palmer's Complete Book of Putting.* New York: Atheneum.

PLAYER, GARY.   1966. *Gary Player's Golf Secrets.* Englewood Cliffs, N.J.: Prentice Hall.

_____. 1967. *Positive Golf.* New York: McGraw-Hill Book Co.

*PRICE, CHARLES.   1962. *The American Golfer.* New York: Random House.

SHANKLAND, CRAIG, DALE SHANKLAND, DOM LUPO, and ROY BENJAMIN.   1978. *The Golfer's Stroke Saver Handbook.* Boston: Little, Brown and Co.

SNEAD, SAM, with DICK AULTMAN.   1978. *Golf Begins at Forty.* New York: Dial Press.

*STEWART, THOMAS P.   1990. *A Tribute to Golf.* Harbour Springs, Mich.: Stewart, Hunter & Assoc.

TOSKI, BOB, and JIM FLICK, with LARRY DENNIS.   1984. *How To Become a Complete Golfer.* Norwalk, Conn.: Golf Digest.

VENTURI, KEN, with AL BARKOW. 1981. *The Venturi Analysis.* New York: Atheneum Press.

*WATSON, TOM, with FRANK HANNIGAN.   1984. *The New Rules of Golf.* New York: Random House.

WIREN, GARY, and DICK COOP, with LARRY SHEEHAN.   1978. *The New Golf Mind.* New York: Simon & Schuster.

WIREN, GARY, with DAWSON TAYLOR.   1987. *Sure Shot.* Chicago: Contemporary Books.

_____. 1984. *Super-power Golf.* Chicago: Contemporary Books.

WRIGHT, MICKEY.   1962. *Play Golf the Wright Way.* Garden City, N.Y.: Doubleday & Co.

INDEX